What Would Your Father Say?

My Journey to Hope and Light

Janice McDermott

*Sandra,
There is only love or fear.
Choose love. That
is all there is!
Love,
Janice*

authorHOUSE®

AuthorHouse™
1663 Liberty Drive
Bloomington, IN 47403
www.authorhouse.com
Phone: 1-800-839-8640

© 2010 Janice McDermott. All rights reserved.

No part of this book may be reproduced, stored in a retrieval system, or transmitted by any means without the written permission of the author.

First published by AuthorHouse 12/13/2010

ISBN: 978-1-4567-2013-1 (sc)
ISBN: 978-1-4567-2012-4 (dj)
ISBN: 978-1-4567-2014-8 (e)

Library of Congress Control Number 2010919014

Printed in the United States of America

Any people depicted in stock imagery provided by Thinkstock are models, and such images are being used for illustrative purposes only.
Certain stock imagery © Thinkstock.

This book is printed on acid-free paper.

Because of the dynamic nature of the Internet, any Web addresses or links contained in this book may have changed since publication and may no longer be valid. The views expressed in this work are solely those of the author and do not necessarily reflect the views of the publisher, and the publisher hereby disclaims any responsibility for them.

This book is dedicated to my loving husband
who has loved me unconditionally.

Table of Contents

Preface xiii
Chapter I: My Father's Death 1
Chapter II: The Orphanage 7
Chapter III: The Foster Home 19
Chapter IV: The Fire 45
Chapter V: The Teenage Years 51
Chapter VI: The Convent Years 69
Chapter VII: From Despair to Hope! 103
Afterword 115
Appendix 119

About the Author

Janice McDermott grew up in a small town in eastern Iowa. She was the second of five children born to parents who had five kids in nine years before her father died. Even though she was not in a family that encouraged dreaming, she always dreamed of writing this story. Even as a child she found herself thinking that her life would make a good story. She has M. A. degrees in Montessori Education and in Curriculum and Instruction, has taught in inner city schools for twenty-nine years, and worked as a Regional Manager for the Colorado Department of Education for eight years. She now  works as a leadership coach, helping school administrators in Colorado and across the country to become the best leaders they can be. She continues her commitment made in the fourth grade to make sure that all teachers in every classroom believe that there is no excuse for their students not succeeding. She has been married for thirty-eight years. They have two daughters who are married and two grandsons.

Acknowledgment

Most authors have many people to thank for helping them make their book become a reality. I have only one person. That person is Debby Bernau. She met with me so many times to edit this book and make my story come alive. I am deeply grateful to her for reading and re-reading and pushing me forward when I found it too painful to continue. Never had I thought that our friendship would include helping me make this book come alive. Thank you. Thank you. Thank you.

Preface

This is my story, the story of our family and what happened after the death of my father. My mother was in love with my father. She did reflect later in her life that it probably was not a good idea to marry a man who had had scarlet fever that resulted in a damaged heart. But she loved my father, so she married him. They were engaged for ten years before they were able to figure out a way to get married. It was the early 1940s. Even arranging to spend time together was very difficult though they lived only ten miles apart; that was a very long way in a horse and buggy. They were both from very poor families who were greatly impacted by the Great Depression.

They were finally married in a ceremony in a small Catholic Church in eastern Iowa, followed by a reception for twenty family members at my mother's parents' house. My Mom wore a knee-length white suit with a white hat covered with netting. They were married for nine years and had five children during their years together. In their tenth year of marriage, my father had a massive heart attack and died instantly. His death so devastated my mother that she could never talk about him without crying. She had completely depended on him, so she became emotionally crippled after his death. Life as we knew it would never be the same. I was the second oldest (age seven) in our row of five children. My youngest brother was only a year old when my father died.

To be clear, life was certainly not great <u>before</u> my father died. He was unable to work. My parents knew that my father's heart was damaged from the scarlet fever he had as a child. Then he had lost his dream right before I was born when an electrical fire completely destroyed his newly-acquired hatchery/gas station. His health issues, in addition to having only an eighth-grade education, meant he was unable to find a good job. My parents were strict Catholics and believed that they must accept all the children God would give them, so they would not and could not practice any form of birth control (other than the approved "rhythm method"). They also knew they could not continue to have children. They argued over how they would feed and clothe these five children with such a limited income--my mother teaching in a one-room school house and my father trying to find work. He pumped gas for awhile. He tried selling Jewel-T products. (Jewel-T was a company that hired workers to sell household goods door-to-door.) He eventually got too sick to work. A doctor they consulted advised them to consider a very risky and experimental type of open heart surgery. The doctors informed them that my father's heart would not last much longer. This was the early 1950s. They had no insurance and no conceivable way to pay for the surgery. They argued about what they should do. They were stressed. They were sent home to make a decision about the surgery. The decision, however, was made for them because my father soon had the heart attack that killed him.

After my father's death, when my mother got upset, she would say to the five of us: "WHAT WOULD YOUR FATHER SAY? He would turn over in his grave if he could see you acting like this. He would be appalled at what you are doing!" This declaration made us all feel very ashamed and guilty. It made us straighten right up. All my life I wondered what my father really would have said. Would he have said it was all fine? Would he have understood that we were just being kids? Would he have understood that much of our fighting was simply sibling rivalry and let us work it out ourselves? Would he have survived the open heart surgery if they had chosen that? Would he have recovered enough to work full time, have had a good paying job and been able to support us? Would he have turned out to be a good father to the children he wanted so badly?

Why my compulsion to tell this story? The only thing I can say is that it feels like my life work. I had it in my mind to tell it even as the drama of our lives was unfolding. I don't pretend to understand this drive to write. I do know that whenever anyone asks me about my dreams, I always end up telling them about my desire to write the story of my life. Even as a child, I remember thinking that I wanted to grow up to make a difference in people's lives! It seems like such a funny thought, but I do remember thinking, "Nobody paid me much attention as a child, but that will be different when I grow up."

At best, I believe that my life story could give others hope. This story might be handed down to my children, grandchildren and great grandchildren to help them understand their ancestors and the courage they exhibited as they lived their lives. At worst, I could write this story and place it in my file cabinet, to be discarded when my oldest daughter, who is efficient and a "thrower-outer" like me, cleans out our home after our death.

Actually, there are a couple of people who got me started on this book. Around 1989, I went to see a palm reader. I am not the type of person who would seek out a palm reader, but I had a neighbor who told me some incredible things about herself and her life. I asked her how she knew about all those things. She told me about her visit to a palm reader in Boulder. I called her immediately and went to see her the next week. She looked at my hands and said, "You are a writer. You need to write your story." I immediately told her that she was way off. She was getting me confused with my older sister. She said: "No!" She assured me that it was me who should write this story. I argued with her but she was insistent. She said my older sister, indeed, had great writing ability, but she was still working on how to connect her head to her heart. She said that I needed to write the story because I realized that connection. She said I could help my sister make this connection by telling this story. She would eventually be successful too, but I needed to lead the way. The palm reader suggested I tell this story to my father. I decided to tell the story a different way.

I came home after the palm reading and started to think about telling this story. Right away, I quickly sketched out some chapters. It seemed so easy for me. I wrote five chapters. These included stories about my life in the convent, my time in the orphanage, my time in the foster home and all the stories I remembered around the time that my father died and my teen years. It had been easy to do and actually turned out to be my first creative experience. I could sit at the computer for hours and not have any idea of how much time had passed while I was reaching into the deep recesses of my brain for the stories.

But, because being a writer was so out of the realm of how I saw myself, I put the stories away. I thought I would get back to them when our children were older, when I had more time, or when they were out of high school. There were so many reasons for me to not dig these stories out of the file cabinet.

I was concerned about what my family would think about me writing and publishing these stories. A book about the trauma we experienced as we were growing up in a little town in Iowa would reopen many of the wounds. We had all done a good job of stifling our pain. We had all developed coping mechanisms to deal with our lives, and I wondered if my family would resent me telling the world about our early experiences. I wondered how the people of my small town would react to hearing the truth about how we were treated when we were growing up. I still have both family and friends living in that small town.

Another concern was that it would force me to face the painful experiences of my life. My life would no longer be my life. It would belong to anyone who chose to read this story. It would force me to deal with the issues I have not wanted to face. I see this as an opportunity to heal, since it brought to the surface emotions that had been buried for so long.

Another issue finally got me to take my writing seriously. I had been telling my close friends that I wanted to write, and had even asked a few people to read the chapters that I had written. They had encouraged me on a regular basis, frequently asking me how my story was coming. I started to notice how badly I felt as I told them that I hadn't worked on it for a very long time. I also realized that my children were now out of high school and college and married. How long would I wait? I needed to get this project underway or stop telling my friends that I wanted to write. I felt like I was a phony. Really, the creative urge is so deep in your soul that you have to do the things you came here to do, no matter what they are.

The "last straw" had surfaced. Since I have begun to seriously write my story, I have gotten sick. Not deathly ill, but I have had more health concerns than at any other time in my life. Over a period of years I went to a chiropractor, an acupuncturist, a hypnotist, a naturopathic doctor, an intuitive, and a natal chart reader. Nothing worked.

As I started to get serious about my writing, I began to feel weak most of the time and in constant pain. I got scared. Maybe writing this story was too painful. Maybe remembering and writing about all those incidents was making me sick. I wanted to stop. However, somehow I realized that there was no turning back. I had never really been sick in my life. Now I could not lift my arms. My chest hurt if I moved it. I was in constant pain, not excruciating pain but a dull pain that is always there. I couldn't ignore it. I went to an internist. She ordered blood work, X-rays and CAT scans. Nothing showed up except some pulled muscles near my sternum. They gave me muscle relaxants that didn't work. How did I pull my muscles? I had no real explanation. I was going to a chiropractor every month. He told me that I had a number of ribs out, sometimes up to eight ribs in the wrong place. Why? I went to an acupuncturist. He said I needed to take it easy. I was putting too much stress on my body. I had blockages between my liver and kidneys, between my lungs and my heart. On and on it went. I came to believe that I must write this story to release these painful memories stored in my body and to deal with all my inner-child issues. I made an appointment to see a therapist who did inner-child work.

I have tried everything to avoid it, but nothing has worked; so here is my story. My hope is that it might help others to heal and help them find within themselves the resiliency that is the hallmark of many children who have struggled during their childhood.

Chapter 1

My Father's Death

His dying on that gray, late October day changed my life forever. It was the end of the fall season. The leaves had completed their glorious cycle of color and had drifted to the ground. The small eastern Iowa town was settling in for another hard winter, a winter that challenged everyone to simply survive. The moment my father had his heart attack, Mom told my older sister and me to quickly take the three smallest children outside. None of us had noticed that there was anything wrong. My older sister and I quickly gathered everyone up. The hysteria in our Mom's voice told us we had better do exactly as we were told. We were used to doing exactly what we were told.

The five of us were sitting on an odd wooden structure, the one that our father was in the middle of building as an addition to the one-car garage. My older sister was holding the baby, who was close to turning two. I was sitting next to my younger brother who was born eleven months after me. I was seven and was holding my younger sister's hand. I didn't want her to fall off the three-foot-high structure. From that spot we could watch all that was happening. We didn't have to wait long because momentarily our parish priest came rushing down the street in his car. He jumped out of the car and raced into the house. We knew it had to be bad if the priest was called first; he would be there to save my father's soul, to administer the last sacrament so that, if he were to die, the blessings of the last rites would guide him straight to heaven where God would greet him with open arms. The second vehicle to arrive was an ambulance. It turned around in the driveway and parked in front of the house. From our vantage point we could not see them carry my father on a stretcher into the ambulance or our Mom climbing into the back of the ambulance with him. We certainly didn't realize that we were being left alone.

It was only minutes later that my Dad's sister, Aunt Delores, arrived at the house. (To this day I do not know how she responded so quickly.) We were told that our Dad was sick and needed to go to the hospital and that we would go home with her. We all jumped into Aunt Delores' old dilapidated car. She had a good heart. She had eleven children of her own so she didn't need five more. But her attitude was: WHAT DIFFERENCE WILL A FEW MORE MAKE? My siblings thought only about getting to play with our cousins out on the farm. I was not thinking that….. I was wondering what was happening to my father. I was the serious child in my family. I knew something serious was underway. I was worried and so was my older sister.

When we arrived at Aunt Delores' house, the older children were preparing lunch. We all sat down on long benches to eat our lunch. There was a long line of bologna and cheese sandwiches being made. There was always room for one more at Aunt Delores' house. We all squeezed together. I knew it would be awhile before we learned how our father was doing. We would have to just wait. We didn't really know Aunt Delores very well. She had her own share of problems, with so many kids and an alcoholic husband. After lunch we were told to go outside to play. As soon as we got outside, I asked my older sister when she thought we would get to go home. I just wanted to sit and wait. She said that we would have to be patient; there was nothing we could do. I watched the long, dirt road, waiting for a car to approach. It was the only way we would find out what was happening because Aunt Delores did not have a phone. Nightfall came but there was no word from anyone about our father. We were all put to bed. There were four of us, all sleeping in the same bed! I did not want to sleep. I tried to stay awake.

That long night was one that I still remember so clearly to this day. I was so worried about my Dad. I wanted to stay awake but my sister said that we would have to wait until morning, so I should go to sleep. Finally, I fell into a restless, fitful sleep but a couple of hours later I woke up needing to go to the bathroom, really bad. Aunt Delores did not have indoor plumbing, so I had to find my way through an unfamiliar house, in total darkness, outside to the outhouse. I got up and started to feel my way to the hallway. I thought I could make it down the back stairs and out the door where the sidewalk would lead me to the outhouse. I groped around, stepping on clothes, falling over shoes, running into walls and finally finding the creaky stairs that would lead me downstairs and outside. Sheer terror gripped me with each step. I had heard Aunt Delores talk about how her house was filled with mice. With every move I imagined that I was going to step on a mouse. I was paralyzed with fear. Finally, I made it outside. Even though I felt good to have made it without an accident, I was equally worried about finding my way back into the same room I was sharing with my cousins and siblings.

The next morning, wearing clothes borrowed from our cousins, we were delivered to school. Aunt Delores said she hadn't heard a word of news so she took us to school as usual. We were only in school two hours when a knock came at my first-grade classroom door. My teacher, Sister Anastasia, answered the door. Somehow I knew the person at the door would be for me. However, I could never have guessed who would be standing there. It was my Uncle Walter, my mother's brother, from Chicago. He whispered something to Sister Anastasia. Her face told me everything I feared! She came back to the center of the room, looking very ashen and called my name. She told me to bring my coat and lunch box and instructed me to go with my uncle. He had my older sister and younger brother with him. He told us that our Mom was in the car waiting for us, with my younger sister and brother. When we reached the car, she told us that our Dad had died. She announced this with little emotion. All five of us sat in the backseat, speechless. What did this really mean? It was impossible for the five of us to truly understand the implications of this astounding information. From school my uncle drove us to the funeral home. We sat in front of the funeral home for the next hour or so while Mom made all the arrangements. We were getting restless and we started to fight. At one point, she came out and yelled at us: "Don't you know that your father has died? Why aren't you crying? Don't you know that you just lost your Dad? What is wrong with you kids?" We had quickly learned how to deal with this news. Our mother was not crying; she was angry with us for fighting. She was setting the tone for how we would deal with his death.

When we arrived back at our house, it felt so empty and quiet! There was something different about the house; something felt very strange.

Very soon another one of my father's sisters came, Aunt Loretta. My father had thirteen brothers and sisters. We were never very close to my father's family, but they did come quickly when they heard he was dead. Aunt Loretta took the three of us girls and my younger brother to her house in a town about fifteen miles away. I think she volunteered to take us because she had money and two daughters about the same ages as my younger sister and me. She was married to a man who owned a feed company. The plan was to loan us her children's clothes so we could look presentable at the wake and funeral. When we arrived at Aunt Loretta's house, we went straight to the girls' bedroom to try on some of the daughters' clothes. The girls did not want to share their clothes. They said to their Mom: "Mom, that is MY favorite dress. Don't give that one to them." They repeated that about everything we tried on. We finally found a couple of cute dresses that fit us. Aunt Loretta emphasized that we were only borrowing these clothes and that we would be returning them. I heard her admonish her girls: "You girls must learn to share and cooperate. These kids just lost their Dad!"

That night we were all sitting around the kitchen table eating supper. The adults were not talking because the radio station, KDTH, was announcing the local obituaries. The radio announcer said: "Vincent McDermott of Cascade, Iowa, died last night of a massive heart attack. He will be waked at the Devaney Funeral Home for the next three days. Friends and family can call tomorrow evening at 7 pm for a rosary. Mass will be said at St. Martin's Catholic Church and he will be buried at the Cascade cemetery." I did not want to look up or take a breath. The silence was deafening. I wished someone would say something. Finally, Aunt Loretta announced we should clean up and get ready for the wake. We had laid out our clothes and taken baths and were ready to go to the funeral home.

We were getting dressed when one of my cousins decided to make a scene. She said she was NOT going to the wake. She did not want to see a dead person lying in a coffin. She refused to get dressed. (She might have been upset because we were dressed in her clothes, but she had so many nice dresses that surely it didn't matter that we were wearing some of them!) She screamed and cried and kept repeating over and over that she would not go anywhere to look at a dead person. Her parents told her that they would make sure she didn't have to look at a dead person.

I stood there, wondering if she could understand that the dead person she was talking about was my Dad!

The wake lasted three days! It was decided that we were old enough and well behaved enough to handle sitting there for three nights, all in a row across from my father's casket. Only my smallest brother was excused from this experience. He was two and couldn't be expected to endure this ordeal. He would join us the last morning when they would actually close the casket and bury him. The four of us sat next to Mom for hours as people filed past the casket. They stopped and spoke to Mom, but very few of them said anything to us. They mostly stared at us from a distance. We could hear people making comments: "Look at those poor kids. What is Helen ever going to do? How is she going to manage? How old are the kids, anyway? They all look so close in age."

In the eyes of a seven year old, I liked seeing my father lying there in the casket. I thought he was just sleeping, lying there so peacefully. He had a smile on his face; everyone commented on that! I didn't like to hear that because that meant he might have been happy to be leaving us. People did say to Mom that he was smiling because that was his nature. He was a good, holy and happy man. To me he just looked the way he did when he was lying on the couch in our living room. I had no idea about the meaning of death. I didn't realize that soon they would close his casket, and we would never see him again!

The next morning that is exactly what happened. We filed by his coffin for one last look. We all stared as my Mom said goodbye to him, and they closed the casket. It was at this moment I realized that he was truly gone. I desperately wanted to cry, but everyone was being strong. I just walked out the back door with my siblings and into a waiting car that would take us to church and then to the cemetery. My older sister took care of my youngest brother during the Mass. It seemed like it took such a long time, but finally we were following my father's casket down the aisle and out into the hearse. All my aunts and uncles and cousins came to the cemetery. We all watched as the pallbearers carried his casket to an open hole in the ground. The priest said some prayers, and then his casket was lowered into the ground. It was over for us. He was gone. Mom was stoic as my Uncle Walter guided her to the car.

We all went back to our house. All of my siblings were sent upstairs to play. It was time for the adults to grieve together. Grandpa (my Mom's

Dad) came up there with us. Grandma had died two years earlier, and Mom said that she was so glad her mother wasn't alive to see her suffer this way! Even though my Dad's parents were alive, they were not part of our lives, and they did not come back to the house that day. Grandpa brought us some good food to eat; a lot of people had donated food. We got out some board games to play. One of the games we loved to play was Sorry! How sorry it was that we were not allowed to grieve or to stay with the adults. We could hear them crying downstairs.

When we were allowed to return downstairs, everyone was gone. Only Mom and five fatherless kids remained. She told us to get on our pajamas and get into bed. The following days were filled with good food and company. My Mom's sister stayed a few days to help Mom write thank you notes to everyone who donated food or gave money for Masses. We wandered around the house listening to the adults talking. We all watched Mom's face, her every movement. We could tell she was overwhelmed and distressed, but she rarely cried. Neither did we!

Gradually things returned to "normal". We did our chores and tried to be good. We tried to cheer up Mom. She seemed to be in a state of shock. How was she going to carry on? What strange twist of fate had landed her in this painful place? This was *not* how she had planned to have her life unfold.

Chapter II
The Orphanage

After my father's death, life changed dramatically. Yes, there were many problems before he died--he had been ill for a number of years and unable to work. He was facing risky major open heart surgery. Although these issues were indeed there, most of the time we weren't so painfully aware of them.

Now, things were different. There was a new tension around the house that wasn't there before. Mom had no one to talk to, so suddenly we were involved with every crisis that she faced. There was always tension in the air. Serious problems seemed to make a daily appearance. We heard Mom crying at night after we went to bed; sometimes she talked out loud to herself. She wondered how she would pay the bills. How would she make enough money to buy shoes and school clothes? What could she possibly do to support her family? How could she afford groceries for five children? Could anyone help her? Could she do it by herself?

She was overwhelmed with the responsibility of raising five small children. Her job, teaching in a one-room school in the country, did not pay enough to support us. My father was painfully aware of the financial problems before he died. He had no insurance and no pension. We were, of course, aware of the financial crisis because my parents' fights were all about money. Mom continued to teach all those years they were engaged but always in a small country schoolhouse. At least, when she was working, my father was home to take care of the two smallest children. Great Uncle Charley, who lived up the street, became our life saver. After my father died, he helped out with taking care of my youngest brother and sister until Mom got home from work.

But Great Uncle Charley was old. He had lost his first wife early in his life, had no children and remained unmarried until he married Great Aunt Agnes later in life. They were to become very important in our lives after my father's death. Aunt Agnes was a wonderful cook. In fact, she was employed as a cook in a nursing home during the week. On the weekends she cooked special treats for us. She helped us celebrate our birthdays and provided a sense of family when no one else was around. We could run up the street to her house when things got crazy around our house. We all did this, including Mom. Great Aunt Agnes's house was immaculate. There was a place for everything in her house and everything had a place. When we visited her we had to sit very still. Her beautiful things were to be looked at only from afar. We longed to play with her black and white ceramic dogs or the tall metal ashtray with the moveable top. That was not to be. The house was always quiet. We were expected to sit still and have a conversation with Aunt Agnes and Uncle Charley. Usually these conversations focused on the birds in the martin birdhouse outside the back door, the flowers growing in the yard or the vegetables sprouting in their garden.

There was another reason we sat so still during these escapes from our stressful home life. Aunt Agnes sat very still. She was very overweight from all her years of cooking (and eating). She needed to rest a lot because her body had to work so hard carrying around all that weight. She did work hard when she didn't have us visiting her. She would be busy cleaning, waxing floors, tending her flowers or canning. She always had fresh brownies, cookies, fudge or angel food cake, another reason Aunt Agnes was overweight. She often gave us a treat when we visited her and Uncle Charley.

My father had died, but my two brothers (they were two and six) were too young to be the father around the house so Uncle Charley stepped up to fill that role. He decided that our house needed painting and he came on the weekends to work on the house. One Saturday he was painting right above the front porch, the ladder leaned against the steps and porch. Mom called him down for lunch but as he started to climb down the ladder, he lost his balance. He fell onto the sidewalk and the bucket of white paint flew out of his arms. The whole bucket spilled onto the sidewalk right in front of the porch. Great Uncle Charley was bruised and sore but the sidewalk took the most abuse. That spattered paint was to remain frozen there all the days of our childhood.

Mom returned to teaching in a one-room schoolhouse. At that time, one needed only a high school diploma and a few college courses to become a teacher. She had taken a college class every summer to qualify. She continued to teach in a one-room school about ten miles from our home after our Dad died. She not only had the responsibility of caring for her own five children, but also that of educating twenty other children ranging in age from six to thirteen. She drove to school on graveled, country roads; it would still be dark when she arrived at school. Her duties included: shoveling a path to the school if it had snowed, starting the fire in the stove to heat the classroom, and being ready for her lessons when the children arrived. If the roads were too dangerous to drive, some of the children came on horseback. At the end of the day, Mom made her way back home to cook us dinner, help us with our homework and get us all in bed. When we were settled she baked bread for the next day. During these late hours she also prepared lessons for her students. She often told us: "Whatever you do, don't become teachers when you grow up! It is a hard life. There is no end to the work."

In one respect, life didn't change that much for us after our Dad's death. A life of poverty and hard work was not new to us. After my father's death we embarked on clearing the plot of land to plant a garden at our home. (When my father was alive he went to his parents' land to plant a garden.) Clearing the land required hard work by all of us. First, we used a shovel to dig up the whole plot which had to be big enough to grow sufficient food for a family of six to make it through the winter. Mom helped us set up the rows with strings so they would be nice and straight. We planted tomatoes, potatoes, onions, carrots, squash, peas and green beans--row after row of vegetables. Through the summer we weeded and weeded; we were well aware of how critical it was to take good care of the garden. We lived off the land, growing everything that we could to ensure a stock of food during the winter months. Those canned vegetables got us through the winter months. In the fall we dug potatoes and onions and stored them in the basement for the long winter months. We raised chickens for their eggs. When the chickens got old and no longer laid eggs, we ate them. On late summer days we scoured the countryside for wild raspberries, gooseberries, blackberries, mulberries and strawberries. We canned these fruits to make jams and jellies. Our own canned fruit was a special treat at the end of a meal.

Sometimes there wasn't enough money for shoes for all of us. Mom's father would come for a visit and help out by taking a couple of us to buy shoes. Mom became an excellent seamstress; she sewed everything we wore, except for our underwear and socks. She also taught us to darn our own socks using a light bulb and darning cotton.

Even with all these cost-cutting measures we still did not have enough money to live. She wondered aloud: "What is going to become of us? What are we going to do?" Soon after my father's death, Mom was visited by a social worker who told her about two programs that could help us. One was called Aid to Families with Dependent Children (AFDC). The other was a food program called Commodities. She knew she had to take advantage of these programs but she was embarrassed. She knew families that used (and abused) the system who had a bad reputation in our small community. She was a proud woman and didn't want to take anything from anyone that wasn't rightfully hers. In her heart she did not want us to be AFDC children. Not only was there a stigma attached to taking money from the government; even worse was that people on welfare were generally considered lazy and unwilling to work. With great humility and sadness, she applied for both programs and finally got a letter of approval.

We were now part of the social welfare system. This meant that social workers regularly checked up on us. My Mom could not make a cent of money without reporting it; if she ever got caught she would lose her monthly payments or have them reduced by the amount that she made. Mom was so honest that any dollar she made sewing a dress or hemming a pair of pants was reported, and that amount was deducted from our check. The food program did enable us to enjoy some of the finer things in life. Every month we were recipients of a huge chunk of cheese, a large can of peanut butter, a couple of pounds of butter and some canned chunks of beef.

It was humiliating for Mom to drive into the city to pick up these food items. When we made these "welfare trips" we also stopped at a discount bakery store in town. Mom would buy a huge bag of crushed bread. The bags said "NOT FIT FOR HUMAN CONSUMPTION".

These bags of bread were sold to local farmers who fed it to pigs to fatten them up. It was always so much fun to split the bag open and see what goodies were stuffed inside. Sometimes, if we got a particularly good bag, there were donuts, cupcakes, and cinnamon bread in addition to regular bread. We would straighten out the bread and re-bag it so we could make sandwiches; sometimes it was so smashed that we simply had to throw it away.

Mom seemed more withdrawn and unhappy as the weeks and months passed. The crush of all the stress was getting the best of her. She lost a lot of weight. At 5' 10" she weighed only 110 pounds. Anyone close to our family surely could have predicted what was about to happen. Mom simply withdrew after my father died. Secretly, she could not believe how her life had unfolded. Part of the problem was that there wasn't anyone close to us. After her husband's death, his family simply disappeared. He had thirteen siblings but only one of his brothers remained close. He and his wife stopped in often to check on how we were doing. He had a farm and a big family of his own, but they were kind to Mom. She really liked his wife. She could always cheer Mom up better than anyone else. She was a lighthearted, happy woman. She told lots of stories that made Mom laugh. They always brought little things to Mom. We loved it when they stopped by because she always felt better after this couple came to visit. My mother had one sister who was very busy with her own life. She did come to visit when she could but she lived a hundred miles away. She had had difficulty getting pregnant so she and her husband adopted a baby. She got pregnant immediately after the adoption so she had two small children of her own. She worked part time as a nurse in a doctor's office; her husband worked in a factory. They were tired on the weekends but they did join us for the holidays. These were fun times because Mom always relaxed with her sister around. They would talk together in the bedroom. I know Mom told her all her troubles.

Mom kept saying she didn't feel well. We started to notice she was coughing a lot. She would cough up phlegm into a hankie, then walk away to look at it. She finally told us about the doctor's appointment. It was very unusual for Mom to go to the doctor; she really did not believe in doctors. We had been raised to believe that if you were sick, you should just lay still, rest and wait for the body to heal itself. The body will heal itself if you just wait long enough. We did not take medicine and neither did she. But she was not able to rest and she continued to cough up blood and lose weight. It scared her enough to make an appointment. It was her sister, who was a nurse, who convinced her that she MUST go see a doctor.

Although aware of this appointment, we could never have guessed how this one doctor's visit would change our lives. We were walking home from school on that fine, fall day. The leaves on the trees had turned their most beautiful shades of yellows, reds and oranges. We were walking along kicking the falling leaves. We had turned the corner to go down our street when we saw an unfamiliar car sitting in front of our house. We didn't recognize the car so we picked up our speed to get to the house quickly. We were greeted by a social worker with an official name badge on her dress. She said that Mom was very ill. She was diagnosed with tuberculosis. She said most people call it TB. She would have to be treated at a sanitarium for TB patients. We could not stay alone, so she was making arrangements to have us stay at an orphanage until Mom was well enough to take care of us again. Our smallest brother was still a baby. The orphanage did not accept such small children, so he would be going to Chicago to live with the same uncle who came to get us from school when Dad died. Mom would be taken immediately to a sanitarium one hundred miles away. We would go to an orphanage thirty miles in the opposite direction. The house would be locked and sealed. Our family would be going to three different places.

There was no need to worry about packing any clothes. We weren't allowed to take anything with us. All of our things had been exposed to TB germs. We all said goodbye to Mom and then climbed into the social worker's car to leave with a total stranger. Not a single tear was shed. My older sister sat in the front seat and tried to carry on a conversation with the social worker. She was ten and "in charge". As we sat silently in the backseat she asked all the questions: When was Mom going to the hospital? Where was the orphanage? When would we get to see Mom again? Would we all stay together? Where was our baby brother going? What about our clothes…… why weren't we able to take anything with us?

Mom was still at the house when we got into the car, but she would be taken to the hospital by ambulance as soon as my Uncle Walter could come to get my youngest brother. He had to drive from Chicago. We were told that our first stop would be a clinic where we would all be tested to see if we were active carriers of TB. We could not enter the orphanage if we tested positive for TB. We waited a very long time for the results of the chest x-rays and the skin test. We sat in silence the entire time. We were too scared to imagine what might happen next. The social worker told us that as soon as the results came back, she would be free to take us to the orphanage. She explained that we would stay there only long enough for Mom to get well. No, she couldn't really tell us how long that would be. Yes, she would bring us back home as soon as Mom was better.

Finally, we received word that, even though we had been exposed to the bacteria, we were all healthy enough to go to the orphanage. We drove up the front drive of the orphanage. It was a huge institution. We were greeted by some nuns who seemed to know a lot about us already. Boys and girls were separated so my younger brother went to the boys' wing. My older sister and I were placed in the same wing, but my younger sister was sent to be with the youngest girls in another wing. We saw each other only at meal times. It seemed strange but we did not have much to say to one another. We simply said "hi" and then were on our way, following the bigger girls back to our wing.

Life in the orphanage was filled with mystery. Every time I met my siblings, during our recreation time, I asked the same questions: Do you know how Mom is doing? When do you think we will be able to leave? Have you heard from Mom? Do you think our relatives know where we are? Will someone come to see us? What has happened to other kids who live here? We felt like we weren't *really* orphans because we would be leaving as soon as Mom was well enough to come for us.

Every day we went to a small school located in the orphanage. My older sister attended a nearby Catholic elementary school. She had a lot of homework. I was in second grade. Even though I never missed a day of school, I was there in body only. My mind was somewhere else. I was not interested in reading or writing or spelling or math. I wanted to know where my Mom was and when I would go home. I don't remember having any homework or even working in class; we sat around and talked a lot during our class time. I had a sense that the teachers felt sorry for us and didn't want to burden us with work either during class or afterward.

We had been in the orphanage for about three months when we had our first visitors. It was a Sunday afternoon. We were called to the front parlor, a room that was off limits unless you had visitors. Our Great Uncle Charley and Aunt Agnes were waiting for us. They brought some of Agnes's wonderful fudge. We sat silently; my older sister did most of the talking. She told them what it was like to live in the "Home". It was called St. Mary's Orphanage but we all referred to it as the "Home". (It didn't feel the least little bit like home.) We asked them how Mom was doing. They had been to visit her. She was very weak and not able to get out of bed. She was doing everything she could to get well so she could come get us. We asked them how long they thought we would be here. They left us with these parting words: "It will take a long time for her to get well. She is very sick." They told us she was not allowed to get out of bed. She was too weak to even write us a letter. This was not good news, but it did help us settle into the routine of the orphanage and accept that we weren't going to be leaving anytime soon. Even though we were not truly orphans, we would have to live as orphans until Mom got better.

It was in the orphanage that my older sister started getting into trouble. The nuns did not know how to deal with her, so they sent her to another school outside the orphanage. She asked too many questions. She was too smart. She had her own ideas about how things should be done. She refused to do something simply because the nuns told her to do it. She was used to being in charge: she had moved into her adult role as soon as Dad died even though she was only nine years old.

It was also at this same time that I learned about the facts of life. I was eight years old. One day we were all standing around outside in the back of the building. All of a sudden a girl by the name of Theola started shouting. She was standing as stiff as a board and refused to move. I kept asking the older kids what was wrong with her. They told me that I was too young to understand. I refused to take "no" for an answer! I followed them upstairs asking them what happened. Finally, in the bathroom they told me that Theola "got her period". That didn't help me at all because I didn't know what that meant. So I kept bugging them until they explained. They said that Theola had never been told about getting her period so she was very scared. When I went back to where she had been standing, I saw blood on the cement.

After that I heard lots of conversation about "getting your period". The nuns in the orphanage yelled at the older girls when there was blood on sheets or clothes. I was so fearful about it, but someone told me that I had nothing to worry about because I was still much too young. All I knew was "it" wasn't a fun thing.

In my bed at the end of a large dorm room full of beds, I lay awake at night, watching a light come through the windows and play across the walls. The search light from a small airport nearby guided planes onto the runway. I pretended the light was held by someone looking for us, saying to myself: "Yes, we are here. Come and get us." The rescuers would climb the walls, and take us away and return us to our home where all my family awaited us. I knew this was just a game in my mind but it was a dream I could not escape. Other nights I dreamt about where that light would lead me if I could follow it. I wondered about what my life would be in that big unknown world out there. The search light both frightened me and comforted me. I was not alone when I lay awake trying to figure out how to get to sleep when I didn't have anyone to comfort me. I had to figure it out on my own so I kept watching the lights.

In my dorm room, I also learned about the "evils" of make-up. The older girls who were going on an outing hid their make-up in their pockets. At the movie theater they went straight to the bathroom to apply it and they might have gotten away with it had they not forgotten to take it off on returning home. The nuns were furious. They all got extra punishments and, from then on, were unofficially labeled the "bad girls". My older sister was not part of this crowd. I was thankful for that. She was not interested in makeup. She had much more important things on her mind.

I was always the good girl: very quiet, didn't want to make any trouble, shy, easy to deal with and did not want to attract attention. I tried to follow all the rules. I was quiet and didn't even ask questions. For my good behavior I was rewarded by being chosen to carry the crown for the May crowning of the Blessed Virgin Mary, as part of a long procession into the chapel. One girl was chosen to crown the statue of Mary. That was the highest honor. Almost as honorable was the second to last person, the one who carried the crown. (That was my job!)

I wore a beautiful long white dress that was loaned to me by the orphanage. My younger sister made her First Communion that same day, so she was also dressed in all white. I carried the crown on a small white pillow. The procession had lots of singing and spring flowers: bridal wreath and lilacs. These were the only flowers blooming in late May in the Midwest. Everyone from the orphanage was there and photos were taken to record the event. As part of the ceremony we all made little shrines of our own, although I do not recall doing anything other than painting them. Someone snapped a picture of the four of us standing with our little Blessed Virgin Mary shrines. We were surviving the orphanage but there was such a far-away look in our faces in that picture. There were no smiles. We were all lost in our thoughts: When would we get to go home? Why isn't anyone coming to get us? Where is Mom? Is she getting better? Where are Aunt Agnes and Uncle Al and their two children? Does anyone know we are in this orphanage?

Our second set of visitors arrived a couple of months later. It was Uncle Cyril and Aunt Viola, the brother to whom my father was the closest. They had become regular visitors in our home to support Mom after my father's death. They gave us the same dismal news: she is resting comfortably but is very weak and confined to bed. Her recovery will just take time. They promised that when she was well enough to come home, they would come and get us. It was comforting to know there was a plan once Mom was strong enough to come home.

During that year I do remember one other set of visitors, Aunt Agnes and Uncle Al. Aunt Agnes was Mom's sister. I was so happy for their visit because they were our favorites. (We also believed they would know best what was happening with Mom.) They did NOT bring their children who were our closest cousins. (We had lots of cousins but none who came to visit us.) I wondered why they didn't bring their children. They were our closest cousins. Were they embarrassed about us living in an orphanage? Would it have scared them? I wondered if they felt guilty to have not taken us into their home. I kept telling myself that I wasn't a *real* orphan because I did have a mother. We were patiently waiting for her to get well enough to come and take us home!

My older sister was not so patient. She wanted to go home. She was getting into a lot of trouble. As good as I was, she was equally bad. I don't think she was really bad; she just became accustomed to being in charge since my father's death. She got into trouble for running in the hallways or saying something inappropriate to the nuns. She was regularly punished for her transgressions by having to kneel **in front of** the chapel. She was too bad to even go into chapel to ask for forgiveness!

It was a lesson in public humiliation. She would be kneeling there as we all filed into chapel. I was so sad to see her there and I just wanted to run away. Why did the nuns have to be so mean? Didn't they know she was sad and angry about her abandonment? Didn't they know she was just playing the role she had taken on as a result of having a mother who was incapable of being the adult in charge? Why couldn't they be kinder to her?

In fact, the nuns did try to help her. They had a psychologist who visited the "home" once a week. I think this guy was hired to help the nuns deal with my sister. She talked to him on a regular basis, but I am not sure he did help her because she continued to misbehave and get into even more trouble. I, too, had one visit with him. I liked going to see him. I must have passed all the "tests" he gave me because I never got to go back. I liked seeing him and wanted to return. I wanted someone to talk to me so I could understand all my thoughts and feelings but I had learned to play the game; I was the good girl and didn't act out, so everyone assumed that I was adjusting perfectly to this situation. (This was so far from the truth. In reality, my heart was breaking.)

Yes, the whole school year passed. I finished my second grade at the orphanage. I had actually missed a whole year of school. Little did I know how much requiring so little work of us because we were "orphans" would affect my academic progress. Letting us play games and sit around talking, instead of doing our school work, did not serve us. We got away with "murder". We used our status as orphans to be very manipulative, employing every excuse in the book to get out of doing work. It worked; the adults in the orphanage fell for our tricks. They felt sorry for us and we used this for all it was worth.

We were approaching our first-year anniversary of being in the orphanage. We were all getting impatient with not hearing about Mom. I would constantly ask my older sister if she had heard anything. Finally, we did get word that we could go home. We would be leaving the next morning. Mom was going to be released from the hospital. Aunt Viola and Uncle Cyril would drive us home after Sunday Mass. We left as quickly as we came. We came with nothing and we left with a few mementos of our year in the orphanage. The clothes we wore would find their way to the next children who came to the "home". Again we waited in the front parlor. All four of us just sat there staring at each other. What would happen next? How would Mom look? We hadn't seen her in a year. What would happen once we got home? Would we be able to keep our family together? The nuns told us that we would need to help Mom because she had been in the hospital so long and was very weak. My older sister and I assured them that we would be able to do that. We were determined not to have to return to the orphanage. One year of our lives in that place was enough. Fear gripped our hearts because we were unsure if we could do what it would take to keep our family together and also make sure Mom got the rest she needed.

It seemed we waited for hours before our aunt and uncle showed up but I doubt it was that long. We were just so anxious to go. However, instead of going straight home, we spent the afternoon on their farm. We ate dinner there; my uncle did the chores and then drove us home. We had waited an entire year and now we had to sit around and wait for my uncle to finish his chores. I was mad but I didn't say a word. I just waited. I tried to play with my cousins but I JUST WANTED TO GO HOME. Couldn't anyone understand that? This day seemed like an eternity as we went through the motions of waiting patiently to be taken home.

Finally we were in the car driving into town. My home town looked strange. It seemed like we had been away so much longer. The biggest surprise was about to come into view as we drove down our street and caught a glimpse of our house. The house looked the same but the grass had not been cut in a year. It looked like an abandoned home. Someone had trampled down the weeds to make a path to the front door. We walked through that path to see Mom attended by a nurse. We gave her a group hug. She looked different; she had gained so much weight because she had been in bed for a whole year. She seemed weak and helpless. The nurse gave us her little speech about needing to be "big girls" and help Mom. It was up to us to keep the family together. If Mom did too much, she would get sick again and have to return to the hospital. (The message was that it would be our fault if Mom got sick again.) We assured her we would do everything we could to help Mom rest and "continue her recovery". We were determined to NOT go back to the orphanage. We told Mom we didn't ever want to live there again. She promised us we would NEVER have to go away again. We all slept well that night. I took such comfort in knowing that I would never again have to follow the landing lights from the nearby airport when I couldn't sleep.

Chapter III
The Foster Home

My sister and I wanted to do whatever it took to keep our family together. This was a big order to fill for a nine and eleven year old. I was starting third grade and my older sister, fifth grade. We took charge of the cooking, cleaning and laundry. Mom was there telling us what to do—a frustrating situation for her. She said that it would be so much easier for her to just do it herself. We begged her to sit down and rest so she would sit and tell us what to do. However, as she got stronger, she didn't listen to us anymore or perhaps she could not stand to see us working so hard. She felt compelled to help so she ignored the warnings of the nurses and doctors.

Our baby brother had grown up during the year he spent in Chicago with his Uncle Walter. He seemed subdued and distant when we saw him after that year. He had become a cute little blond-headed boy who was nicknamed "Whitie". We all wanted to pick him up and carry him around but he would have no part of that. He had grown so independent. Only if Mom wasn't around would he go to my older sister.

Our home was located in eastern Iowa close to the Mississippi River. Because of the climate and humidity, the grass there continues to grow green and lush well into September and October. Three seasons of the year, spring, summer and fall, the grass required mowing every week. We had left in late summer so the grass had grown for almost a year. Now we had returned in June to see our home surrounded by weeds and overgrown grass. It was an overwhelming task but was the first thing we had to do once we arrived home. We all took turns with the scythe--chopping, slicing, and cutting down the weeds; our old push mower was useless in such high weeds and grass. Once the tall grass was cut we went over it again and again with the push mower. We had over a half acre to mow by hand. This seemed like an endless, thankless task. We worked on it every day. After two hours of work, only a small area was cleared, but it was important to us to return our house to looking like someone lived there, like we had come home. My younger brother suggested we buy some sheep and have them eat the grass. That was a great idea. We could also shear their wool every year to sell for cash. Mom bought four sheep. Every spring the shearers would come, and Mom sold the wool in the closest large city. In return she received enough money to buy us some of the things she could not make herself for the coming school year.

Doing the laundry was yet another huge challenge that we had to face once we were all back together. We spent all day *every Saturday* doing the laundry. First, we heated the water on the stove, and then we poured the hot water into the old wringer washer. As the machine washed the first load, we heated more water for the rinse tubs; the first rinse tub removed the soap from the clothes, the second tub was to whiten the clothes with bluing. (That never made sense to me--adding a blue liquid to the water to whiten the clothes--but it seemed to work because the white clothes were whiter after that tub.) Then we scrubbed all the socks with a bar of special soap for really dirty items. Our hands turned red and raw from the scrubbing. As I stood at the sink scrubbing the socks, I often wished that somehow, white socks would go out of style; any dark color of socks would have been so much better, but the fashion at the time was white and we all had white socks.

We put every piece of laundry through the wringer one by one after each rinse. After the third wring they were ready to be hung. In the spring, summer and fall this was no problem. Winter was another story. Winter presented us with a whole new set of challenges. Winter in Iowa is brutal, with temperatures frequently 20 below zero and a wind chill factor of 30 or 40 below. The wind swept across the fields blowing and drifting the snow. We didn't have extra clothes; so we couldn't skip a wash day. No matter what was happening outside, we would wash. The first step in doing winter laundry was to dig a path through the snow to the clothesline. That allowed us to run outside with the wet clothes in the basket to the line. The clothes would often freeze before we could hang them on the lines, as did our hands. Our hands got so cold that we would run through the snow into the house to warm our hands, then run back to finish. The clothes would hang there "stiff as a board" as my Mom would say. We argued with Mom: How could they dry if they were already frozen? Somehow they did. If it started to snow we put on our boots and heavy coats to run out and get the stiffened clothes off the line. We stood them up in the kitchen and after a few minutes they started to thaw and crumple onto the floor. We had only one drying rack, so we used every available spot in the kitchen and living room to drape clothes. These were the only rooms with heat; the kitchen had a wood burning stove, the living room, an oil burning stove.

One of the biggest problems we faced on laundry day was disposing of all the dirty water. Carrying all the buckets of dirty water outside was too much work, and we spilled lots of water. At one point my brothers got creative. (Getting rid of the water was their responsibility.) They found some old downspouts and gutters from the side of the garage, hooked them all together and attached the washing machine drain to the downspout/gutter system they had created. It was pretty ingenious and we were all excited when it worked well. Usually some water would spill but it flowed pretty well through the downspout into the gutters that snaked their way through our kitchen and out the back door! Then there were times when, for no apparent reason, one of the gutters tipped over causing a huge flood in the kitchen. We were all called into service to grab the rags from the rag box and start wiping up the water. It usually caused a ruckus and we would all laugh at our failed attempts at "saving time".

The next stage of the laundry process was mine exclusively. First, I filled the 7-Up bottle with water. This 7-Up bottle had a special cork top with lots of tiny holes on it and I used it to sprinkle all the clothes. It was important to get the top on tight or the clothes would be drenched with water. On occasion the cork came loose, and I would get very upset and have to return the clothes to the line. I sprinkled every item of clothing, rolled them up and placed them in a plastic-lined basket to be ironed. I couldn't wait too long, or they would start to mold. It was crucial that I put enough water on them; if not, I would have big wrinkles that would not come out when I ironed them. We ironed everything--sheets, pillowcases, tablecloths and all our clothes. There were reasons that I did this job exclusively. One was that I hated to cook. If I was ironing I didn't have to cook. Another reason was that I was always cold. The iron warmed me up. Ironing made me feel good. Besides, I was very good at ironing. Actually, there was yet another reason. If I was ironing I was in the kitchen with mother. I needed to be close to comfort her. We could talk. I was vigilant in my companionship with my Mom. I tried to say things that would help her cope with her life. I would encourage her, console her and reassure her that things would work out. Mom always felt bad that we were working so hard. My two brothers hung out together and my two sisters were good buddies, so I was the middle child. It was the role I played in my family.

After finishing the laundry, we scrubbed the large linoleum kitchen floor on our hands and knees--and waxed it with Johnson's Wax--a job that seemed to take forever. After my Mom's illness my older sister and I had taken over the task of making bread. Setting the bread to rise in a sunny spot in the kitchen, we waited until it had risen past the top of the bowl, and then punched it down to rise again. From the dough we made loaves of bread, dinner rolls and cinnamon rolls. Cinnamon rolls were the best. After rolling out the dough with a rolling pin, we sprinkled butter, sugar and cinnamon on it and then shaped it into a long cylindrical roll to cut it into slices. These slices were placed on a pan to rise and when they were high enough, baked in the oven. We always wanted a fresh roll when they came out of the oven, but Mom gave us only the end pieces. The good rolls were to be consumed on Sunday morning after church when we had a big breakfast of eggs, bacon and the rolls. It was so good! Sunday was a day of rest when, depending on the time of year, we would do different activities. In the summer and fall, we went on picnics to gather berries or nuts. In the winter, we went ice skating on a rink next to the park across from our house.

During this time I got reacquainted with my best friend, Donna. She was a wonderful friend. She was lively and cute and never lacked for great ideas for fun things to do. I had been gone for a whole year, so she was very excited when she learned I was home. The first time she came by the house, she asked me to come out and play. I sadly told her that I couldn't come out to play because I had work to do. Mom overheard me saying this, and she told me that I could go out and play with her. I felt weird, being home and seeing my friends after my absence. I had been through so much. How could I tell her all the things I had experienced when she really didn't seem to want to know? She just wanted to take up where we had left off. I wasn't the same kid, but she didn't know that. I complained about how much work we had to do. She told me to stop feeling sorry for myself and just get playing. She said I acted like I was the only one with problems which angered me because I truly thought that she had no idea what my life was like or how I was feeling. After all, she did have the perfect family (or so I thought at the time). Her father worked as a delivery man for the Texaco Oil Company, delivering oil to all the homes in the area with oil burning stoves. He often drove past us in his big red delivery truck with the Texaco sign on it. Sometimes he would stop to say "hi". If he could, he would give us a ride home from school. The best part was that the truck had a small box of red suckers sitting on the passenger-side floor board. He always gave us a sucker when he stopped. It made us feel so special to walk down the street with those red cherry suckers in our mouths!

My older sister was working doubly hard. She had the most responsibility for making sure things did not fall apart. She was our mother when Mom was not able to be present, either physically or mentally. She fought all the battles Mom was too weak to fight, such as taking on the nuns at school, the electric company and the traveling salesmen who often preyed on my mother. This job fell to my sister.

At one point Mom was notified that my younger brother would be put in special education classes. He didn't get a good foundation during his first grade year in the orphanage. He was in kindergarten when he lost his father so he really "missed" his first two years of school. (Like me he was never absent but was often not there mentally because of the emotional trauma he was experiencing.) The nuns decided that because he was behind, he should be put in classes for "retarded" students. Well, my older sister would hear nothing of the sort. She marched right up there and told everyone that her brother was not "retarded" and that NO ONE was going to put him in a class that would damage him even more. She had watched him take over as the man of the house. He was able to fix everything mechanical: he had taken apart the lawn mower and put it back together so it worked perfectly. He had fixed the car when it broke down. My sister could see he was so gifted mechanically. And with no one to teach him, he taught himself.

Gradually, Mom was up and around and working harder than she should have been. She proclaimed that we were not strong enough to do some of the chores so she had to do them. Kneading the bread was one of them. She baked bread every other day. It took a lot of strength to knead the bread, and she would have coughing spells when she was working. We all begged her to stop, to buy the huge bags of bread at the discount bakery. We now had another reason to buy the bread. Uncle Cyril had given my brothers a couple of runt pigs. If my brothers could keep them alive we would take them to market with Uncle Cyril's pigs. So we really did want some of the bread for the pigs--the parts that were too crushed to eat. But mostly we had the great pleasure of eating the soft white bread that was store bought!

It was tense at our house. There were just too many obstacles to overcome. We were struggling to keep everything from collapsing but we were so glad to have a roof over our heads and to be all under the same roof. In one of the few instances that Mom mentioned Dad, she said that one of the best decisions he ever made was to purchase the house right after their marriage. He had great plans for that property. There was the hatchery with a gas station attached, potentially a great source of income to support the family. This dream was short lived, however, because the hatchery burned to the ground just days before I was born. Both Mom and Dad were thankful that everyone in the family was safe and that no one died in the fire. Even though the property was only one block from the main street of our small town, the hatchery burned to the ground because there was no fire hydrant on that street and the volunteer fire department could not respond quickly enough. The water tower sat at the top of our street, but that didn't help. After the hatchery burned, plans were made to transform the other side of the property into a roller skating rink, another potential money-making venture. The trenches were dug to build the rink but my father's lack of funds and his poor health put these plans on hold. The grass eventually grew, providing lovely sloping hills for the sheep to graze. These trenches always represented for us my Dad's unfulfilled dream.

It was around this time that I realized my Mom had never wanted any kids, and here she was "stuck" with *five* kids. Mom felt she wouldn't be a good mother for even one child. She said that it was my Dad who wanted a big family. She was angry for the situation she found herself in: this was **not** how she thought her life would unfold. She was getting more and more depressed, but she couldn't give up. She had five children, all totally dependent on her. When her sister came to visit she would just cry. Her sister was a nurse, so she would tell her to rest more, to relax. This advice fell on deaf ears. There were clothes to make, mouths to feed, money to be made.

Sunday was the one day of the week we did not work. Our preparations for Sunday started on Saturday night. The cinnamon rolls were made. Now we all needed to take a bath. First, we heated the water for the large tub that was set on the kitchen floor. The kitchen then became off limits to everyone except the person taking a bath. The kitchen was the warmest room in the house because of the wood-burning stove, so it was the best place to bathe. We all used the same water, so it was very good to get to go first! The oldest was first and I was second. (There were some benefits to being almost the oldest!) We did have a tub upstairs, but since it only had cold water, we didn't really use it. With no heat upstairs, we also dressed for bed in the warmth of the kitchen.

We each had one good Sunday church outfit, made by Mom. These outfits were worn only on Sunday morning when we went to Mass. As soon as we got home from church, we went immediately upstairs to change so they would stay clean and in good shape for the next church service. She sewed our outfits in the evenings, attempting to keep up with us as we grew. Sewing was luckily one thing that Mom could do without a lot of exertion. It was important for her that we looked good for Sunday Mass.

As a child I was fascinated by the rituals of the Catholic Church. We NEVER missed Mass. That service seemed to be an island of calm in our stressful lives. We prayed that God would help us, would look favorably on us, and would be there for us. It seemed however, that God was moody and silent. I wondered how we could convince God that He needed to help us. Couldn't He see we were in trouble? Why was He so silent? Why did other people seem so lucky? I believed there must be some magic formula that I just needed to learn. Mom believed that we must strive to be the best Catholics possible; if we did our part, God would be good to us. That included attending every single service offered by the church…… daily Mass, Stations of the Cross, Novenas, Confessions every Saturday, etc. We had our pew and nobody else sat in that pew. We were all expected to behave in Church and we did.

Although we were "making it", there was clear evidence to anyone close to our family that Mom was barely hanging in there. The problem was that there *was* no one close to our family except Mom's sister who had her own problems. She lived ninety miles away and worked part time. Mom went every month to get a checkup at the TB Sanitarium. We dreaded these monthly checkups because we knew that if her chest X-rays showed evidence of TB, we would be in big trouble again. We had seen Mom coughing and spitting up blood. Our fears were well founded.

The worst was exactly what happened. She returned from a doctor's visit to tell us that her TB had come back. She would be forced to return to the sanitarium, but one not too far from our home town. We realized the thing we dreaded the most was about to happen to us again. We were still too young to stay alone without a parent. God only knows how they figured out where to send us this time, but it was decided that we would go to foster homes rather than the orphanage. How would they find foster homes for all of us? Would we be close together? The social worker came the very next day to tell us that they had made arrangements for each of us. We would each be in different homes except for my youngest brother. He would stay with my older sister. He had already been traumatized by his stay in Chicago with an uncle he didn't know. This time he would be with his oldest sister who really was his main caretaker since our Dad had died.

The same procedure was followed. Mom was taken to the sanitarium in a city only twenty-five miles away. We were all taken again to the clinic to be tested for TB. By this time we were deathly afraid of doctors. All during my childhood, I had a recurring problem with fainting: when I got scared I would faint. Because I was so scared, I was afraid it was going to happen now. I prayed that I wouldn't faint. I didn't want these strangers to know how scared I was. We all had chest x-rays and the TB test in our arms. If we had a reaction, we would have further tests. After we were told the good news, the doctor asked to see me again; I thought he was going to tell me that I had TB. I hadn't noticed that I had red splotches all over my body. He told the nurse that he thought I had chicken pox. I tried to convince him that I was just nervous. He was sure that I had the chicken pox, and that my foster parents should be told that I must stay home from school for a week to recover.

This seemed more than I could take. I was going to a foster home where I would have to go immediately to bed for a whole week while I recovered. I didn't feel like God was hearing me so I didn't even ask for God's help with this situation.

As we waited for our test results, we were told about our foster homes. I found out I would go to a foster family in a town twenty miles from home. I was to live with the mayor of the town, who already had three little girls. Surely, he didn't need yet another little girl. These girls didn't need any more competition!

I found out very quickly about my new family because the social worker took me straight there from the clinic. The house was small; I slept in the same room as the three daughters. There were two sets of bunk beds and I was assigned the lower bunk of the beds closest to the door. I wondered if the mayor had taken me in for political reasons; I might have invented this story because the truth is that no situation would have made me happy. I was shy and distant and just wanted to go back home, so perhaps, I didn't give them a chance.

I was miserable at the foster home. For the first time in my life, I started getting sick. After recovering from the chicken pox, I started complaining about one thing after another. First, my legs hurt and then my stomach hurt and then my head hurt. My foster Mom took me to the doctors, but they never found anything wrong with me. My symptoms were real. I really did hurt. I remember sitting on the examination table, the doctor trying to guess what might be making me sick. I thought to myself: "You just don't get it. I want my mother. I will get well as soon as I can go home and be with my Mom." Nothing else would get me well. I was sure of it. I did not share this with my foster parents. They continued to try different medicines and continued to be frustrated with not being able to figure out what was wrong with me. I put them through a lot, but I also was going through a lot.

My younger sister's foster home was not far from mine. I think she was too young to go to school because I don't ever remember seeing her there. She seemed unaffected by the situation our family was facing. She liked her foster home. She was the only girl in a home with three boys, and she quickly turned into a real tomboy. She was so cute and had a great personality; they all doted on her. I heard how much she loved being with that family.

My younger brother was placed in a foster home with a brother and sister who lived on a farm, in the country not too far from the town where I was placed. Neither of them had ever had children or spent much time around children. I don't remember seeing my brother during that year we were foster kids. At some point he got sick too. He was diagnosed with rheumatic fever and placed in a hospital hours from our hometown. I don't remember being told that he was sick. I was so focused on my own situation. I only learned about his illness when he did not return home with us.

I did get to see my older sister and youngest brother. They had been placed with an elderly couple who were not able to have children of their own. They lived on a farm within driving distance of my foster home. They needed help with the farm work because they were getting older--a couple of kids to gather eggs, clean the barn and help with the chores sounded good to them. This couple shopped in the town where I was living and once a week came into town for groceries. The house where I was staying was a block from the grocery store, so I would watch for their arrival each Saturday. Sometimes my brother and sister were with them, and other times just my sister was there. Whenever I got to spend some time alone with my sister, I always told her how miserable I was. She told me she was sorry that I felt so bad. She was facing her own misery and was plotting to run away. But she couldn't run away without taking our brother too. She knew that if she went down the country road, one of the neighbor farmers would come along on a tractor, pick her up and take her right back there. This childless couple did not know how to deal with a preteen and a small child. They had no understanding of the trauma we had faced and the failure we felt at not being able to keep our family together. We had tried so hard and yet we found ourselves scattered all over the countryside in different situations.

Going to school was painful for me--I was so shy. My classmates were friendly, but I felt so alone in the world. I tried to play with a few children at recess, but I never felt like I could ask anyone to come to my foster home. I would be doing fine and then, all of a sudden, I would remember where I was and that I had no idea where my mother was or when I would ever see her again. I got sad and stopped playing.

One of the best things about this situation was that my foster home was right across the street from school, so I could run home for lunch.

My foster Mom was a stay-at-home mom so she had lunch ready for us every day. We had peanut butter and jelly sandwiches she made with fresh, soft white bread and a glass of cold milk with a couple of cookies for dessert. I always wanted such a lunch at home but Mom always made the homemade bread that you couldn't cut into nice even slices. I always wanted a mom who was at home to make our lunches and to talk to us when we came home from school. I had it now. That made me happy even though it wasn't my real Mom. I always delayed leaving the house after lunch so as not to face returning to the playground. My foster Mom always reminded me that it was time to go back, but I waited until I heard the bell ring to run across the street.

I had become a master manipulator. I made sure my classmates and teacher did not ask me to do anything. They knew I was sad and therefore not capable of doing the same work as others. It worked like magic again. I simply had to sit quietly and not respond. The teacher would skip me; the kids would say to each other that I was a foster child. That was my excuse for not doing what was required of other students.

Did we get to visit our Mom that year? The answer is YES. We were picked up one spring day by a social worker who drove us to visit Mom in the TB sanitarium. It had been nine months since we had last seen her. In the lobby of the hospital, we sat there speechless, as a nurse wheeled Mom toward us. We didn't know what to do or say because, again, she looked so different. She had gained so much weight, lying flat on her back in bed all those months. What could we say? Where to start to tell our Mom what we had experienced the past nine months? There *was* nowhere to start to express how traumatic this second period of separation from her was, so none of us said much. Our older sister was the communicator. She asked the question we all wanted to ask: When would she be well enough to go home? (None of us complained to her about our foster homes. In fact, we didn't say a word about them because Mom was telling us how wonderful it was for these families to take us in.) She told us she was getting better and thought she would be released some time in late spring or early summer. That was enough for us. We returned to our foster homes. I told myself, again, that I wasn't really a foster kid because my Mom was coming to get me! (Just like I had convinced myself that I wasn't an orphan because I did have a real Mom.) Every day I waited to hear the news that I was going home.

As the end of the school year approached, I realized that I had managed to complete third grade without doing much of the work. On the last day of school, I was walking home with a young girl I had started making friends with, so I told her that I would not be returning to the school in the fall because my Mom was finally recovered enough for us to all go home. Again, Aunt Viola came for us. She picked up my two sisters and my youngest brother but not my brother closest to me who was confined to a state hospital with rheumatic fever. He was truly the "man of the house". It felt terrible not having him there. My Mom told us that we would visit him as soon as we could.

The arrival home this time was not as traumatic as before. We had grown accustomed to returning home after being gone for a year. The grass didn't seem quite so long. Our friends came by the house, and everyone knew we were home again. No big deal this second time around. Our Mom said: "Yes, you can go out to play until it is time to make dinner." or "No, you can't go out to play because today is our wash day." We picked up where we left off. There was, however, one difference now. Both my older sister and I knew that we would NEVER again allow ourselves to be separated. We knew in our hearts that we would NEVER tolerate a social worker coming to our house to tell us she was taking us away. We felt we were now old enough to be really in charge of running our home if our Mom was too sick to help us.

The week after we got home, Aunt Viola picked us up to bring us to visit my brother at the hospital. All five of us climbed into the car and headed for Iowa City to visit him. We were not allowed to enter the hospital. Luckily, he was in a room on the first floor. We waited patiently for Mom to signal to us so we would know at which window we could see him. We had to stand on our tiptoes to see him through the window. He shared a room with two other patients but none of them looked like our brother. That young boy in a bed in the corner surely didn't look like him, but that was indeed where Mom was standing. He was way too chubby. He didn't say much, so we couldn't really tell if it was him. He seemed so weak. Where was the brother we knew? It was very puzzling and upsetting at the same time. We wondered when and if he would get better and how long he had been in the hospital. We were all silent on the ride home. We had all wanted to see him but seeing him only made us feel worse!

Sometime during the summer he was released from the hospital. He was not able to take on his role as "man of the house" at this point because he had to be very careful as his heart grew stronger. Mom said he needed to be outside to get sunshine and fresh air. He was not able to walk and too heavy to carry so we pulled him in the wagon. We looked forward to the day he could resume his role as a main contributor to the work that needed to be done. It was a delicate balance, and he was absolutely needed to keep everything in balance. He was nine.

Janice's parents during their ten-year engagement.

Janice's parents' official wedding portrait (parents are on left, with best man and maid of honor).

Parents' tombstone

Janice's First Communion, standing in the living room of the family home.

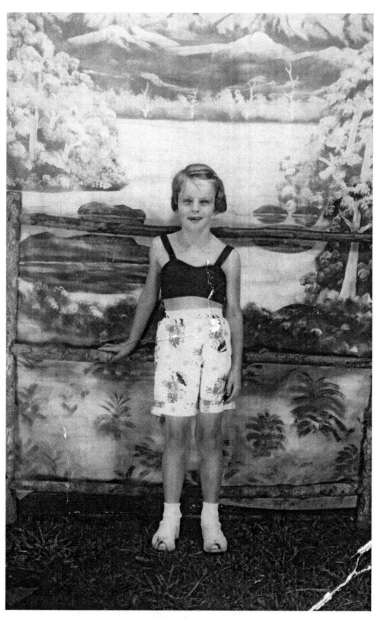

Janice, age 7, right after her father's death.

Janice, age 8, wearing her first store-bought dress.

Janice (in the front, holding the tray for May crowning) accompanied by four girls making their First Communion, including her younger sister (second from left).

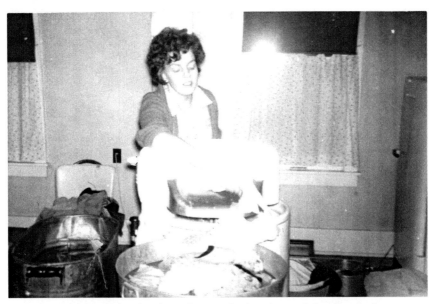
Janice doing Saturday laundry in the kitchen of the family home.

Family home in Iowa in 1962, showing side yard
and future site of the roller skating rink.

Janice (wearing her second store-bought dress) and friend at their convent farewell party.

Janice on the day she received her "sister name" and habit (on lawn of the Motherhouse).

Janice's first visiting day as a postulant
(Janice, her mother and four siblings).

Janice, dressed in wedding gown as a bride of Christ, to receive her habit.

Janice after receiving her habit in the Motherhouse chapel.

Chapter IV

The Fire

After our return from the foster homes, we quickly settled into a routine, doing our chores and making sure that Mom didn't work too hard or get upset. Mom seemed better, rested and stronger. She knew well she needed to take it easy in this second recovery period. This time it didn't feel like there was a sense of impending doom around us all the time. The issue of not enough money was ever present--how to stretch it to pay our bills and have money for food. She often talked to us about money, saying she didn't see any way out of this life of poverty for her. In this small town your fate was determined by what family you were born into or whether you lived on a farm where you could raise cows or pigs to sell. (Every time we drove by a farm that really stunk, she would say, "That is the smell of money.") Lacking one of these two advantages, your only option was to marry a man who had a lot of money. She emphasized that it was important for the girls in the family to get an education so we could support ourselves. She had learned herself that you could not depend on a man.

She kept us on the straight and narrow by reminding us that if we misbehaved she would get sick again and be forced to return to the hospital. It was a very effective way to keep us in line. But we were kids, and we were frustrated. We were unable to deal with everything that had happened to us or with trying to be adults when we were still kids. What we did do was to act out our frustrations by fighting. We fought a lot; actually we would beat on each other. We would scream and cry and scratch each other. We would chase each other through the house with every intention of trying to kill each other. Mom didn't know what to do with us. She would get out the yardstick or the belt and come after us but she just wasn't strong enough. When she started coughing, we would freak out, knowing it was us again making her sick. We truly believed her illness was our fault because she couldn't deal with five children. She had said she didn't want even one child, and now she had five children to contend with all by herself.

Other times she used "psychological force" to control us. She would send the two siblings who were fighting outside in the dead of winter to work it out. This process took forever because we were stubborn and refused to admit we were wrong. It was always the other person who caused the fight. My brother and I might decide to get along, but the minute we stepped back into the house, we would start fighting again. Mom would send us right back outside, asking us and herself, "What would your father say?"

Another effective method for dealing with all the sibling rivalry was to just walk out. She strode up the street to visit with Great Aunt Agnes and Uncle Charley. We fell into silence as soon as she left. We would watch their house as long as she was up there to make sure she was really going to come home. We definitely had a fear that one day she would walk out and never come back; after all she had left us for two years in a row. I always experienced a tremendous sense of relief upon seeing her walking back down the street. In defense of Mom, we really fought a lot. We didn't know how to deal with what the fates threw our way--the discrimination of poverty and the insecurity of having no security.

Mom tried hard to create a life for us. But after lying on her back for two years in the hospital, she was not only physically weak but emotionally crippled. She believed herself to have been victimized by everyone and everything. She couldn't sort out how it was that life had dealt her such a cruel blow; this was not the way she had envisioned her life. She often lamented that there was no way out of this life of poverty. She was depressed and she often cried with the most desperate of sobs. None of us knew what to do. I prayed that someone like Aunt Viola or Aunt Agnes (her sister) would visit and cheer her up. We all got very quiet when Mom was like this. I tried to stay nearby so I would be there just to talk to her, to comfort her, if only I could figure out what to say.

That first Christmas after our return from the foster homes produced a visit by a Catholic priest from a nearby parish who said that his parish had collected Christmas presents for all of us. This priest was not from the parish where we attended church but from my grandparents' parish. He not only brought presents but also a basket of food for us. We were all so happy! The biggest surprise that Christmas was that we all got a bike to share. Santa had dropped it off at our next door neighbor's house by mistake! Our neighbor was an elderly man who was way past the bike-riding stage. We were all thrilled when we saw the bike. Even though we were experiencing a typical--below zero--snowy winter, we found a path through the snow on the pavement in front of the house to practice learning to ride. All four of us wanted to ride. We could not believe our luck to finally have a bike. We all stood in line waiting our turn. Our youngest brother was still too young for a two wheeler so we shared the bike among only the four of us.

The spring after we got our bike, my older sister decided to give my youngest brother a ride on the back. He sat on the bike seat as she pedaled down the blacktop just beyond our house. All of a sudden my brother started screaming. My sister jumped down off the bike to see that his right leg was caught in the spokes of the wheel. He was still little enough to be carried so she rushed him into the house. We all came running because he was screaming so loud. Mom knew immediately that he had a broken leg. Mom drove as fast as our old car would go, to the nearest large city where there was a clinic. My brother screamed the whole way. (It was the same clinic that we had visited for our TB tests and chest x-rays the past two years.) We sat in the car while Mom carried him into the clinic. It seemed like we sat for hours while they put a cast on his leg. When they returned we asked Mom if we could sign our names on his cast; she said we must wait until we arrived home to make sure the plaster was completely dry. My baby brother fell asleep, exhausted from all the crying. My older sister felt terrible about the accident. She started to take special care of him again. She carried him everywhere. He liked this. He wanted only her to carry him.

Somewhere around this time we got indoor plumbing. We continued to use the outhouse in the summer because it was more convenient when we were outside playing. We also had problems with the pipes freezing in the winter, so we didn't really use the bathroom in the winter. Instead we would use a bucket that sat in the bathroom, taking turns each morning to empty it into the outhouse. That was NOT a fun chore. A particularly embarrassing episode happened to me at the outhouse but it is too soon to tell that story.

We were "making ends meet" by planting a huge garden every spring, canning large amounts of produce during the summer, and raising chickens that generously gave us plenty of eggs every day. Every spring the local feed store gave away baby chicks. They did this so customers would then buy feed for the chickens. We kept ours in a make-shift pen on the floor of the kitchen. We enjoyed picking them up and petting them. They were so soft and fuzzy. Mom didn't like us to pet them too much because she thought handling them might make the chicks get sick and die. It was critical for us to keep them alive to produce the many eggs on which we depended.

At some point they got too big to stay in the kitchen and were moved out to the shed that sat on the front of our property. The shed was originally a gas station but it was never used that way. It stood in front of the hatchery but remained standing when the hatchery had burned to the ground. We used it every spring to keep the baby chicks safe and warm. One night Mom heard that the temperature would fall below freezing, so she plugged in a light bulb close to the floor so the chicks could stay warm. She had done that a number of times before. In the middle of the night we were awakened by Mom's screaming. We looked out the window. The whole side of the house was lit up. The shed, our chicken coop, was on fire. The winds were blowing the hot embers directly onto the house. Mom was screaming for us to stay in bed. Given the pitch and intensity of her screams, it sounded like she should be telling us to GET OUT of the house. She did, indeed, mean to tell us to GET OUT, but she was so frightened that she was confused and was saying STAY IN BED. Uncle Charley came to the rescue. As we watched the fire burn out of control, he ran up the stairs and yelled for us to come downstairs right away; he knew the house was in danger of catching on fire. We were downstairs and outside in a flash. We watched as the chicken coop burned to the ground. We all stood there, praying that God would spare us our house. What would we do without a place to live? The fire department was at the scene but the same tragedy as before was repeated. We were less than a block from the water tower, but with no fire hydrant close to the house, there was nothing the volunteer fire fighters could do except watch it burn to the ground. They used what little water they had in the truck to put out the embers that were falling on the house. We stood out there for hours with the firemen. Finally they said it was safe for us to go back inside our house. It took forever to fall back asleep that night.

The next morning came all too soon. We were exhausted, but Mom insisted that we go to school. None of us had recovered from the trauma, but we stumbled down the stairs and climbed into our school uniforms. We instinctively knew we were to act as if nothing had happened. I was still shaking. Everyone at school knew we had had a fire. News like that travels very fast in a small town. When the fire whistle blew, everyone came out to see where the fire was. Even if they hadn't heard the news, everyone knew because all our clothes smelled like smoke (so did our whole house). None of the kids said a word to me, but I desperately needed someone to tell me that things were going to be okay and that they knew what I was going through. Instead, I remember standing close enough to hear two of the nuns talking on the playground. They were talking about our family and all the tragedies we had experienced and "what a pity it was". These situations were helping to form some career decisions that I wasn't even aware of at the time.

This experience made me deathly, irrationally afraid of fires and would be the subject of scary dreams and nightmares for years to come. It was the combination of the hatchery burning a few days before I was born and the chicken coop burning in the middle of the night that made me fear fires so much.

During those years following our stay in the orphanage and the foster homes, we were adjusting to not having two parents. I was becoming painfully aware during this time that a child from a one-parent family that lived in poverty just didn't have much status. This was especially apparent at school. Nowhere else would I experience the level of discrimination I encountered at school. Those children whose families invited the nuns to dinner in their homes or brought them presents for the holidays were treated so much better. They were given the special privileges. The nuns were not discreet in their rude comments about my shoes or about my clothes or the fact I didn't have the supplies I needed. I felt invisible as they talked about me and my family. Maybe it was because I was so quiet or that I was a mediocre student that the nuns felt they could ignore me. I was not a trouble maker. I worked hard. I tried my best, but I was much too worried about the dramas at home to be able to focus on school.

Chapter V

The Teenage Years

There was no stopping life. I was growing and maturing and now in middle school. There is no other way to say this--school was becoming harder for me each year. I had attended a K-8 school so there was no trauma about leaving the security of my elementary school to go into middle school. I just moved next door to the sixth-grade classroom.

What I noticed was that my school work became more and more difficult. I was not a good reader; I had trouble comprehending what I was reading. Reading was so painful. For reading instruction we each took a turn at reading out loud. I did not attempt to understand what was being read because I spent every minute trying to figure out which paragraph would be mine to read out loud by counting the number of kids before me. As the other students read out loud, I practiced my paragraph. I would panic if I saw words I didn't know. I would try to ask someone sitting next to me. Sometimes I would mispronounce a word and everyone would laugh. I remember mispronouncing "depot"; I said DE-POT. It seemed like the whole world was laughing with a mighty roar. I'm sure it was just a few students snickering, but I was so fragile that it seemed everyone was making fun of me. I developed a phobia for reading out loud. The teacher announcing that we would be reading a story out loud was enough to ensure that I would have no comprehension of the story.

Another situation that caused me great pain in school was going to the chalkboard to diagram sentences. We took turns. I always prayed that somehow I wouldn't get called. I hid behind other kids in the hope the teacher wouldn't see me. Standing in front of the group made me so nervous that I couldn't concentrate at all on what I was supposed to be doing. The nun gave each of us a sentence to diagram, which we would write on the board and then draw lines to indicate the parts of speech. I worried about not remembering the whole sentence, about spelling the words wrong, about how to diagram the sentence, and finally, about putting the words on the right lines. I must say though, by eighth grade, I did get somewhat proficient at diagramming sentences.

Reading was hard for me but math was even more difficult. No matter how hard I tried, I could not remember my times tables. No one ever taught me any strategies for remembering them. I knew my 2's and 5's by heart but that was all. I did, however, invent a way to compensate for not being able to remember them. I had a notebook filled with white lined paper. On the cardboard back of this notebook was a grid with the times tables and all the equals measurements. I cut out the times tables grid and carried it with me for years sneaking a look at it when needed. Keeping track of the grid wasn't as difficult as you might think. We wore the same navy blue pleated skirt and white blouse uniform every day. As we had only one uniform each, it was always in my pocket!

Nothing in middle school was as painful for me as spelling bees. I practiced my spelling words every week and did pretty well on spelling tests, but spelling bees were way too much pressure. I was so shy that feeling everyone look at me while I tried to figure out how to spell a word was more than I could handle. I needed to write the word down to see if it looked right. Lined up with all the kids in my class, I always misspelled the word on the first try and was always humiliated when I had to sit down.

Another absolutely impossible situation for me was an assignment to memorize a poem or the Preamble to the Constitution. I just couldn't memorize anything; I had no clue about how to do it. I simply told every teacher that I couldn't memorize. I was pretty convincing because they all let me get by with not having to do it. One teacher insisted that we ALL had to recite the poem. I kept telling her I wasn't ready to do it yet. Finally, the whole class had done it but me. She finally told me privately to recite my poem to one of my classmates instead of the whole class. I was ecstatic that she let me off the hook, but then I realized that she also excused another student who was obviously very slow. I decided that I must be as dumb as the really slow kid in my class. The classmate who listened to me recite the poem was very smart and wanted to show off; she recited whole lines for me instead of making me do it myself.

My penmanship was excellent and I figured I got that from my Mom because she had excellent penmanship. I was always proud of how she wrote the notes to my teachers. Learning how to write creatively was the difficult part. I remember begging Mom to help me. The assignment was to write a thank you letter to a friend or to write a paragraph on a topic; I had to make it all up. I sat in the kitchen and cried. Mom felt sorry for me and, in total frustration, finally told me exactly what to write. She was angry that I couldn't do it by myself and said I should be able to write something that simple. I had convinced the whole world that I was helpless and not capable of doing anything academic. Everyone around me came to my rescue. During this time I also became a masterful copier. I did not hesitate to copy anyone else's work. My classmates knew this and covered their work so I couldn't copy but I still tried. I had totally convinced myself that I was not able to do the work myself. I had no reason to believe anything else.

Another tragedy, involving my best friend, came during my middle school years. She told me she had a "dreadful" secret to tell me. Before recess the whole class walked single file down to the basement to the bathroom. My friend and I were last in line. (I am not sure how we managed this because we were not allowed to sit together.) We had planned it this way so she could tell her secret to me in the bathroom stall, where no one else would hear. Her parents were getting divorced, and she was moving away with her Mom and her siblings. I was devastated! How could I lose my best friend? What would I do for a friend now? She was the only one I really liked.

I rationalized: she was quite popular and wouldn't like me for much longer anyway because she was starting to get interested in boys. I was not able to deal with the boys' teasing. I was not cute. Yes, it was best for her to leave. BUT, it was such a loss. I had fun with my friend. She was the one person who could make me forget my problems. She was so engaging that I completely forgot who and where I was when I was with her.

I remember the year she decided to throw a Halloween party. We went straight to her house after school. She and her older sister and her Mom were there and had all the supplies. We immediately got busy setting up the basement for the party. We had a big tub that we filled with water and tested to make sure the apples floated on the top. We hung scary things all around. We cooked some spaghetti and covered the bowl, planning to put the bowl behind a curtain and tell all the kids they were feeling slimy dog guts. We were having so much fun that I totally lost track of time. I heard my friend's Mom calling me from the top of the stairs. Her voice had a pitch that alarmed me. I ran up the steps to see my mother at the front door. She was very angry with me and worried about me. She hadn't known where I was and it was dark out. I told her I was sorry, but I got involved in helping my friend get ready for the Halloween party. All the way home she yelled at me for not being responsible. I needed to come right home every night! Didn't I know that she had four other children at home alone? Didn't I know she needed to be cooking dinner for us instead of running around to all the neighbors asking if they had seen me? I don't actually remember the Halloween party. All the fun was erased as I decided that I was a bad girl and that I should not have a good time but remember my responsibilities.

One of the last things we did before my friend moved away was to play together in a field down the road from our house. She was a free spirit and loved doing things that I knew would get me into trouble if Mom found out about them. That is what made her so fun. We both needed to go to the bathroom. She said we could just pull our pants down and go right there. I knew I would get into a lot of trouble for doing this, but she said that there was no one around and she would never tell anyone, so we just pulled down our pants and peed together. We were in a neighbor's field because my friend wanted to ride his horses. We were trying to catch them to pet them and see if we could ride them. Of course, I was scared of the horses but she was determined to ride them. The horses ran away so we just lay down in the middle of the field on the green grass. We were lying there when we saw a plane way up in the sky leaving a trail of white vapor. We wondered where that plane might be going. We both decided we would grow up to be stewardesses and travel the whole world. I felt like there was a chance I could actually do that when I was with my friend. She let me dream and she believed that it would happen for both of us. But she was leaving me and I didn't know when I would ever see her again. My heart was so heavy.

Another issue that I started to deal with was my teeth. We never had toothpaste and were not taught to brush our teeth regularly. As a result we had really bad teeth. First, we didn't brush often and when we did we used baking soda. Secondly, we didn't go to the dentist because we couldn't afford to go until we started having a toothache. When I did go to the dentist, I never took Novocain because either our dentist didn't believe in it or it cost too much, and I was afraid of shots. Years later, I heard that part of my issues around decaying teeth was that, because I never had Novocain, the dentist could not drill deep enough to get to the bottom of the decay so my teeth all rotted underneath my fillings.

My two brothers really missed doing things that needed a father during these years. They were "fatherless" when it came time to practice baseball or join Boy Scouts. There was no man around to talk to them about what it meant to grow up to be a man or to role model being a good father. My Mom worried about who would talk to them about the facts of life.

However, even without this role modeling, my brothers were stepping up to the plate to be "the men in our house." They were learning how to take apart the lawn mower, fix what was broken and put it back together. They were learning how to fix the car when it broke down, how to do plumbing and electrical work. Actually, anything that needed to be fixed on our property could be fixed by them. One time Mom decided that an old tool shed needed to be taken down; both my brothers and younger sister took the whole thing down. There was nothing they would not tackle.

My sisters and I were suffering too from not having a male figure around. We struggled with how to relate to men. I, particularly, was so shy around boys, I couldn't even look at the boys in my class. I was so scared of them. They teased the other girls in class, but they rarely said anything to me. I felt too uncomfortable to talk to them. I felt invisible around them. My friends were starting to have crushes on the boys, but I watched it all without having any idea of how to relate to them.

After my friend moved away I looked for a new best friend. There was nobody that I really liked. I tried to be friends with a girl up the street who shared the same birthday as me. She was not nice to me and, in fact, would routinely be mean to me. One of the things that hurt me the most during this time was that she had a birthday party and did not invite me. It was my birthday too! All my classmates were up the street at her house.

There were three of us in my class who celebrated the same birthday. She invited the other friend, but not me. I was devastated. I even asked my friend why she didn't invite me. She said that the invitation must have gotten lost in the mail. I didn't fall for that excuse, not for one minute. I knew she didn't like me and really didn't want to hang around with me. The problem was that every single day, I had to walk right by her house in order to walk to school. Often she was coming out of her house just as I was walking by, so I frequently ended up walking with her.

I had been babysitting since sixth grade for the neighbors who lived up the street. Every year they had another baby. By eighth grade I was already dealing with three babies. I got paid 35 cents an hour and I saved every penny I made. I would fall asleep soon after I got the babies settled, and when the parents arrived home, I was still sound asleep. They had a hard time waking me up. I wondered if they were concerned about my sound sleeping. I was so exhausted from the day's work that staying up late was out of the question for me.

In eighth grade I became a nanny for a baby who lived in a house up the hill from my school. I climbed the hill after school, taking charge of the baby so the Mom could have time to herself. The house was beautiful. The view was beautiful, overlooking our small town. I took the baby out in the carriage for a walk and to sleep in the shade under a tree in the backyard; the Mom had put a net over the baby so mosquitoes wouldn't bite her. My job was to walk the baby until she fell asleep; then I would sit and watch her sleep. If the baby was asleep in her crib when I arrived, I would be assigned cleaning chores. I dusted, mopped, vacuumed and cleaned the bathrooms. I got a chance to see how the other half of the world lived. It looked like a wonderful life.

One Saturday evening I was minding the baby after spending the day by the river with some friends. We had laid out all afternoon in the sun. I had fair skin so I knew I had gotten burned. I put some lotion on my burned skin. I had the chills, but as soon as I got home I was picked up to go babysitting. It wasn't long before I started feeling sick. I was trying to take care of the baby and throwing up at the same time. I was dizzy and fainting. I just sat down with the baby when I felt faint. Never once did I think I should call my Mom. I needed the money so I would stay there. The next day I told Mom how sick I was. She said I probably was experiencing a sun stroke because I had spent the whole day in the hot sun.

During my eighth-grade year I also got my first real job--at Ray's Drive Inn. My older sister worked there as a carhop. I was so shy that I just wanted to work in the kitchen cooking the orders. I was very excited to get this job. We got regular working hours and every night after our shift we would get to order anything we wanted off the menu. That was the best part. Although it was only open during the summer, I was ensured of having something to do all summer long. I always worked the night shift, guaranteeing that I would get home late and that Mom would let both my sister and me sleep late. We were required to get up early until we had this excuse.

The first official night that I worked at Ray's, I was assigned to washing dishes in the backroom. My task was to ensure a constant supply of frozen mugs. First, I washed the mugs in the sink and then put them on a rack in an opening in the wall. When they had dried I put them in the freezer so they would be cold and frosty when the root beer was served. After I had washed my first set of dirty mugs, I started to pile another set on top of the first set. Somehow, one of the mugs fell off the rack and straight down into the cooler, which was inconveniently open, where it shattered into a million pieces. The whole cooler had to be turned off and defrosted, while all the frozen mugs were washed again to remove the glass shards. I was mortified. How could I go back to work at this drive inn? I wasn't even capable of washing dishes without creating a huge problem. I went home thinking that they probably wouldn't ever have me back. But I did go back the next night, and for all four years of high school--ALWAYS being very careful when washing those mugs.

My very favorite items to order at Ray's were beef tenderloin or a fish sandwich with fries. Both were deep fried. I just couldn't bring myself to eat a hamburger because I probably cooked one hundred hamburgers each night. I prepared coleslaw and potato salad when we weren't busy. I also made the batter for onion rings. They were so good but, even then, we knew they weren't very good for us. After we closed for the evening we ordered our food and ate as we did the closing chores--sweeping the floor, cleaning the catsup and mustard bottles, filling the salt and pepper shakers, and scrubbing the grill. That was by far the worst job; often Ray or his wife would do it. Then they would drive us home, basking in the knowledge that we made some money and had some good food to eat.

The drive inn also had an inside cafe, where I waited on those customers too. That was, for me, the hardest part because I never felt comfortable making change. The old-fashioned cash register didn't calculate how much change to give back to the customers. I would be cooking an order when fifteen people would arrive expecting to be served. I found this a huge challenge. The owners were great about covering the cooking while I waited on those customers who had chosen to come inside to eat, usually when they were busy outside. They probably thought they would be served faster if they didn't have to wait for a carhop.

As I matured the changes in my body began to frighten me. I was embarrassed because my breasts had started to develop. One of them was normal but the other was not developing properly. Mom insisted I start wearing a bra. I didn't want a bra. I remember always wearing something over my blouse. Even when it was very hot I would wear a sweater. I will never forget the first day I wore a bra. Some kids in school teased me about it. From that day on, I slouched forward to mask the fact that I was developing breasts. I could tell how uneven they were. I imagined that everyone was gossiping about my breasts. One time when my Mom's sister was visiting, she had me show my breasts to my aunt who was a nurse. They both stood there looking at me like I had five tits instead of two. They agreed that my lack of development had something to do with the fact that I had suffered from malnutrition when I was a baby. At that time I had almost died, spending days in the hospital while my doctor attempted to find a formula that would stay down. I was allergic to a number on the market but never was it suggested that Mom breastfeed me. From that day forward I felt like I was a freak of sorts. I was so embarrassed about how I looked that I now wore my bra everywhere, even to bed. I didn't want anyone to see my breast. I refused to undress in front of anyone.

Getting my period was painful too. It arrived at the absolute worst time: I was in the middle of getting ready for a style show at the county fair. I was in 4-H and was to model a dress I made. Mom had never said a word to me about getting my period. I only knew about it because of the incident that had happened in the orphanage. I had already decided that I would not tell my Mom when I got my period because she had never even talked to me about it. The night before the style show, I was awakened by a rumbling in my stomach. I thought I had wet my pants so I ran to the bathroom, where I discovered a huge clot of blood. I was in a panic. I stuffed toilet paper in my pants and raced to the back closet where Mom kept all the rags. I knew that was what I had to use, but I had never walked with a rag balanced between my legs. What if it fell out of my pants when I was modeling my dress? What if the rag wasn't big enough and blood stained my dress? This was not bad enough. Yet another style show disaster awaited me.

Mom had sent me with her friend to the next town to buy a pair of shoes for the style show as I didn't have any good shoes. She dropped me off in front of the only shoe store in town. I had never shopped for shoes before so I didn't have a clue about my size. I don't recall whether the salesman measured my feet, but I definitely walked out of that shoe store with a pair of white patent leather shoes at least one size too big. I could not walk in them without my heels slipping out. I tried to hold them on by gripping my toes together. When I showed Mom the shoes I purchased, she was horrified. How could I have bought a pair of shoes so obviously too big? What was I thinking? It was too late to return to town so I had no choice but to wear them. I guess Mom figured I might grow into them in a year or two. Maybe that was what I was thinking too.

I went to the fair with my 4-H leader. I acted strange from the beginning of the trip. I was so afraid that when I sat down the blood would show through my outfit that I tried to hold myself up off the backseat of the car. The kids I was with didn't seem to notice. When we arrived at the fair grounds I went straight to the bathroom, not real bathrooms but cement stalls set up just for the fair. I went so often that the leader asked me if I was feeling okay. I replied that I didn't feel good, but she was so preoccupied with getting the others and their outfits ready for the show that she didn't pay much attention to me. That was good because I spent most of the time going to the bathroom to check my make-shift pad. I had no idea what my body was doing, but it sure was inconvenient and messy. I didn't like it at all.

Finally, it was time for me to model my dress. It was a very light shade of blue organza with darker blue flocked flowers on the see-through material. I was proud of the dress I had made, but I just knew that my Mom had helped me way too much. She had become an excellent seamstress out of necessity. She made me rip things out, as many times as needed to ensure the dress looked really good. Yes, the dress looked good but that was it. My new shoes slipped on every step as I climbed the stairs to the stage. I slid them across the stage so they wouldn't come off as I walked. Judges were scoring us on our outfit but also on how we walked. I walked carefully and climbed down the steps on the other side on the stage--all without falling. It was over. I didn't care what score I got or if I got a blue ribbon. I had only one thing on my mind: I had my period and I needed to go immediately to the bathroom to check to see if things were still okay.

The biggest problem was that I didn't want Mom to know. I was obsessed with hiding this fact. It took a lot of vigilance for me to hide all the evidence and make sure she didn't see any clues, including taking the rags to the trash to burn. I didn't sleep well during my period; I was worried I would get blood on my pajamas or, even worse, the sheets. Well, I hid it successfully for over a year. Mom started to fret and threatened to take me to the doctor. I told her to be patient with me. I figured that if she didn't want to tell me about getting my period, she didn't need to know when I did.

Finally, one morning it all fell apart. We were doing the wash and Mom asked me: "Have you gotten your period?" I said "no". Then she showed me my pajamas. I told her that it had just happened but I didn't want to tell her. The secret was out.

When I reached ninth grade, my Mom and I went to register at the new Catholic high school, built the year before for the five surrounding communities without a Catholic high school. Parents wanting a Catholic education for their children were required to bus their children to this school. There was absolutely no question in my family that we would all continue our education at the new school. (There was no public high school in our town; it was ten miles to the closest public school.) We had this option because our family paid on a sliding scale according to our income. My older sister had attended and I had heard lots of tales from her. I was very nervous about going to high school. Even though I always did my homework, worked hard and rarely missed a day of school in the last eight years, I already knew high school would not be easy for me.

I remember Mom helped me to fill out all the registration forms; this was followed by an oral interview with the principal. I was told that I would be assigned to the "C" class where the material covered would be "appropriate" to my abilities. At that point, I had no idea what the "C" class meant. It was just what my Mom expected; she was convinced that she had really dumb kids. When asked: "What are your hobbies?" I told her that my favorite hobby was to iron!!!!! Mom was mortified and yelled at me as soon as we got into the car. "Why did you tell her you loved to iron?" Honestly, I couldn't think of anything else and that was how I had spent most of my time outside of school. She told me that I must have some hobbies!!!!!! I asked her what I should have said. What were my hobbies? I didn't know and neither did she.

My freshman year of high school, I finally made a new best friend. Her name was Marian. She lived in the country on a large farm, had a huge family--thirteen brothers and sisters--and her life seemed as difficult as mine. They had the tiniest house I had ever seen. Her Mom and Dad slept in the living room and entering the house, we walked right through their bedroom. (I did wonder: how could they make so many babies with everyone walking through their bedroom? I figured out that by the time the kids were coming home late at night, they had stopped making babies.) There was a large kitchen in the back of the house. It produced the best tasting down-home cooking you can imagine. Here bread was baked, delicious apple pies were made, and food from the garden was canned. A curious sight was a very tiny room off the kitchen, where the kids sat and fought while waiting to be called for dinner. With only two bedrooms upstairs, the boys all slept in one and the girls in the other (two double beds and a couple of fold-up cots in each room; that was it for the house).

My new friend and I had a lot in common. She was poor, although I thought she was rich because they had a large farm and lots of animals. She had to work hard, though, maybe even harder than me because there were so many kids and such a small space to keep them all. We immediately became best friends. We talked for hours on the phone. This was a problem however because our one and only phone was on a small piece of furniture near the front door in the living room. There was no privacy. Everyone heard our phone conversations, and people on our party line up and down the road could listen to our conversations too. Mom got exasperated with me because I stayed on the phone for hours. We saw each other every day at school but we still had so much to talk about when we got home. Mostly, we talked about our lives. We were trying to sort them out. Our little sisters gave us a great deal of grief. We both agreed that they should be doing more to help out, that they were both the youngest girls and liked their special status.

How I loved visiting this farm! I learned so much about life there. In fact, I learned everything I needed to learn about life on this farm: how to make babies and how to drive. My friend and I talked about how you get pregnant; she kept saying that our parents did the same thing as the cows. I didn't know what the cows did! I had never noticed them doing anything like that before. I did not believe her, but she took me to the barn and showed me. She showed me other wondrous things such as: how to milk the cows by hand, how to separate the cream, and how the milk was stored so that the dairy company could come and get the milk, pasteurize it, put it in cartons and deliver it to the stores for me to buy.

Learning to drive turned out to be a real challenge for me. First, we had a very old car--a 1947 stick shift Chevy born the same year as me. Mom did not let me drive out of the driveway while I was learning to drive, so all I did was drive forward and back in the driveway. I never got out of first gear and reverse. BUT my friend's house was a different story--an old car and acres and acres of land to drive on! I must have killed the car a hundred times as I tried to shift from first to second gear. Her whole family watched this crazy scene, starting, going forward, and coming to a jerking stop and then starting over. I could not stop laughing as I attempted to coordinate one hand on the wheel, left foot on the clutch and right hand on the stick shift. Part of the fun was how much I laughed. It took a long time and much patience from my friend before I was able to drive successfully across the fields. She was lucky, she had been driving a tractor and watching her older brothers and sisters learn, so she seemed to have no trouble with this skill.

My friend also made friends with a few other kids in her classes. She was in all the higher-level classes and she invited some in her class to join our group. I did not make friends with anyone from my classes. I was in the lowest group, and there was no one in my class that I could relate to. The boys just clowned around and made life hell for every teacher. They were fulfilling the expectations that were set for us: we were all slow, and there was really no hope for us to achieve anything other than the bare minimum.

We created our own little clique since we didn't seem to fit in with any of the other cliques in our hometown. We were not popular. We didn't seem to have what it took to be with the "in" crowd. We could never figure out why we didn't fit in. We just knew we didn't. Even though we were not the "in" crowd who got all the guys' attention, we did have lots of fun together. We were wild and silly and crazy. We laughed uncontrollably about the simplest of things. One of us would start laughing and then we all would go crazy with laughing. All five of us had this in common: problems that we needed to escape. One of our friends had some very out-of-it parents and seven brothers with a baby sister born later in life. She convinced us that her parents were crazy. Another friend had wealthy parents who gave her everything but never what she really needed. Another of our friends had an alcoholic mother who created havoc every day when she got too drunk to take care of the seven children.

During my freshman year I found a job taking care of the mother of one of my Mom's friends, who was in the advanced stages of Alzheimer's disease. She did not want to put her mother in a nursing home. In fact, I do not believe there was such a thing where I grew up. She wanted to take care of her Mom, but it was a very taxing job so she hired me to assist. She picked me up early every Saturday morning, with me exhausted from hanging out with my friends late on Friday night. Once at her house, I would just sit. It was pure torture for me because the house was so hot and the woman couldn't carry on a conversation. She didn't know who I was. She was very confused. When the whistle blew each noon she thought it was a fire and tried to escape from the house. Often it was so quiet for such long periods of time that I would fall asleep. When a noise awakened me, I would jump up and race around the house searching for her inside and outside. My main job was to ensure she didn't wander away. I was petrified when I couldn't find her. When I finally did locate her, I had to coax her back to the house by promising to fix her lunch even though it wasn't lunch time. Once again, I renewed my vows to never fall asleep again. It was a constant battle to stay awake; the quiet and the heat, paired with nothing to do, ensured I would nod off. One time I fixed her lunch but she couldn't find her teeth. I looked everywhere. I always monitored her because she did really silly things: this time I found her teeth in the freezer. This job lasted a whole year. I needed to make money so I couldn't afford to turn down a job. Finally, the woman died and I was freed from going to that crazy house every Saturday!

I also babysat for a young couple with two small children. I particularly liked going to this house because I found a booklet on a bookshelf that explained the facts of life. Every time I went there, I would read and reread it after I got the children to bed. I read that sexual intercourse was required to get pregnant. I wasn't quite sure what that meant. I also read that if you missed a period you were probably pregnant. I knew mine should be coming. In fact I thought I should get it that very night. All night I kept checking. I was sick from worrying about it. I didn't think I could be pregnant, but I didn't have my period. What could I do? I figured that I would just have to wait to see if I started getting bigger. I didn't even think to talk to my older sister; we were not close during this time.

My older sister and I were not close because we really had nothing in common. She was outgoing, loud and smart, had the leads in the class plays, was a cheerleader and was good at everything she did. It seemed that I was just the opposite. She did try to help me. She encouraged me to go out for cheerleading, and she tried to teach me the routines for the cheers. She encouraged me to try out for plays. I was too shy to even work backstage as the prompter. She tried to help me with projects. One time I entered a poster in a contest. I won the contest, but all my friends said: "Your big sister drew that poster, didn't she? You should not have accepted the prize because you didn't do the work! We know your sister is good at drawing. This is not your work." I was humiliated and decided not to ask her for help again. She took all the upper-level classes. She was good at everything except one thing--getting along with people. She was accustomed to being in charge. It worked well at home but not with her peers. When she would tell them what to do, they got mad at her.

Even though we weren't particularly close, my older sister saved my life, and to this day I am grateful for her help with this particularly thorny situation.......... One morning I was running late to get to school; I forgot to go to the bathroom. As I left the house I remembered that I had to use the bathroom, so I decided to just visit the outhouse instead of going back into the house. That would have been fine, but that very day my older sister had asked me to return a friend's Mother's diamond ring to her at school that morning. I was wearing the beautiful diamond on my ring finger. (My sister had the ring because my friend was on the same cheerleader squad. They had cheered a game the night before. She had given it to my sister because she was afraid she might lose it while she was cheering.) My sister had given me specific instructions about making sure I returned the ring as soon as I got to school. As I was wiping my butt, the ring fell off my finger and disappeared into the dark piles of shit far below. I panicked. What would I tell my friend? What could I tell my sister? Where would we get the money to buy another ring? The worst of all, now everyone in my class would know that I was still using the outhouse!!!!

I ran into the house and confessed to my sister what had happened. I was hyperventilating. She told me to calm down and go on to school; she would deal with it. I did what she said but all day I was sick with worry. How could I admit that I had lost the ring? All day long I didn't want to talk to anyone; my friends asked me what was wrong. I was too embarrassed to tell anyone what happened. I felt like crying all the way home but I did not cry. I saw no way out of this dilemma. As soon as I walked into the house, my sister told me that she had **found** the ring! I couldn't believe what I was hearing! HOW? She told me that after I left, she went out to the garage, found an old fishing rod with some wire and used a flashlight to look down the hole. Once she spotted the ring, she was able, after *many* attempts, to fish that ring right out of the pile of shit. She had cleaned it up and told me that SHE would deliver the ring to my friend. After that she often joked about the "diamonds in the privy"!

I did date during high school but I was so nervous on every date. I would literally stop breathing. It was never about having a good time. I was uncomfortable being with any male; it didn't matter who it was. I was nervous about how I looked, what to talk about and where we went. A movie was the best choice, but I was always afraid my date would want to *hold hands*. Mine were always cold and clammy. Eating out was difficult too. To combat my fears, I always ordered the same thing: shrimp, fries and a Coke. Shrimp was easy to eat, and I could eat both the shrimp and the fries quickly with my hands and then focus on what I should be saying. I didn't like it when my date looked at me. I felt self conscious. I always worried about the possibility of having to kiss the guy goodnight. I almost always responded by suggesting that we should wait to have our first kiss. (I am not sure what I was waiting for....) I once asked a friend what she said when she didn't want to kiss a guy. She said "we should wait" so I said the same thing!!! I later heard that my nickname with the guys in our class was "freezer". It certainly fit me.

One Sunday we found ourselves in the church choir loft, preparing to sing for a Mass, with no adults to supervise. Of course, we were all messing around, laughing and tickling each other and falling off the pews. When my sister heard all of us up in the choir loft, she marched right up there and told us all to be quiet. She said that if we couldn't be quiet we should just leave. Some of the girls (the nuns' favorites) got mad and told the nuns that next day that my sister had been yelling at them. One of the nuns took my sister out of class and marched her to each classroom to apologize to the kids for her behavior. My sister refused to apologize so they just stood there. She believed she had nothing to apologize for and refused to do it. It was very bold and unheard of to defy a nun. I was so embarrassed by my sister's defiance. I had certainly learned my lessons well: we were to be seen but not heard. We were to do exactly what the nuns told us to do. I was the good girl and did exactly what I was supposed to do because that would keep the peace and not make trouble for my Mom. My sister believed that the nuns treated us differently because we were poor. She complained bitterly to Mom about this inequality of treatment.

One really happy memory from this period of my life was that I had a couple of friends who loved to dance and we would practice at their houses between dances. During dances we simply didn't care what anyone thought. We danced every dance. Dancing was fun and if boys didn't ask us, we danced with each other. We did this shamelessly.

My high school years can be divided into two periods. The first two years were spent trying to figure out how to be popular and well liked. I watched the other girls and tried to imitate what they did so I could be popular too, but it never worked. I had a very bad feeling about myself being in the "C" track along with all the kids who were "losers". It was the lowest track. I fought this designation from the beginning. I wanted to take Latin and Algebra. They said no. I kept worrying about how I could get an education if the nuns told me that I couldn't take certain classes. In my sophomore year I convinced the nuns to let me take both Latin and Algebra. All my friends had taken these classes the year before so I was with the freshman class. I had no friends and nobody to talk to or help me when I was struggling in these classes. I barely made it through both classes. I never won this battle during high school because I was always a year behind with the classes I was taking. I did get to take Geometry but no other higher-level math classes. In the end I graduated with the lowest group. I was never able to convince anyone that I didn't belong with this group of kids. In fact, at this school, once you got into the lowest group, there was never any discussion about being able to get out of it.

The second period of my high school life began around the start of my junior year. I sensed a very distinct difference about how I felt toward life. I had now seen for years the hopelessness of living a life of poverty in a small town. There was no chance of getting a date with the boys in my class who were popular and had money. There was no way to escape the unwritten "caste system". I also began to think about what I would do when my eighteenth birthday came and I would no longer be eligible for AFDC assistance. I looked for a way out of this closed system. One thing I knew for sure is that I had to leave this town and never come back. How could I do that? My family was still there. At this point I shut down as a person. I gave up. I stopped wanting to go to dances. I wanted to work all the time so I didn't have to deal with the rejection I felt. My friends started to say that I had changed. I stopped laughing like I had my first two years of high school. I stopped thinking everything was funny. In fact, very little was funny anymore. It was hard to keep going, but I did arrive at one decision, one that I shared with no one.

I had identified a few options for my future. For example, I could become a hairdresser or a secretary, or marry a farmer. None of these sounded like anything I could see myself doing. So I rejected them totally. I had decided that there was only one way available to me to escape totally: I would go to the convent. It was brilliant. It was a very honorable option because I grew up in a totally Catholic community of Irish and German Catholics. It was not a difficult decision because it was truly the only option I could come up with. I felt that I was too ugly to ever get married. I decided that I could never have children because I was too frightened of doctors and hospitals to ever voluntarily go there. Also, I never wanted children because we had been told that children made your life even more miserable. The main reason the convent sounded good: I could get an education. There was also my indoctrination to the belief that God is a very unpredictable, hard to satisfy sort of father figure. Surely I would not go to hell if I dedicated my whole life to Him.

Chapter VI

The Convent Years

I was the tender age of seventeen when my Mom started to really pressure me to make some decisions--about what I would do when I turned eighteen. The cause of her distress was that my Aid to Families with Dependent Children check would disappear when I turned eighteen. She could no longer afford for me to live at home. I turned eighteen in January but didn't graduate until June, and I wouldn't leave until September if I went away to school. I had been working during high school, saving my money in a bank account. I wasn't making much money; my jobs paid so little. (My regular babysitting job paid 35 cents an hour.) I could have helped my Mom with grocery money, but we never had that discussion. I put every cent in the bank because I knew I needed to be on my own as soon as I finished school.

Well, it turned out to be a pretty simple decision. I used a process of elimination to figure it out. It became clear to me on our senior class retreat. As part of the retreat we were required to meet with the priest to discuss our post-graduation plans. I announced that I thought I was being called to the religious life. We discussed how one would know this. He directed me to pray about it. I didn't really feel I needed to pray about it. I was so certain. I had this gut feeling that it was the right thing to do: God was calling me to enter into His service. I also thought I would bring honor and respect to my family; Catholic families that had a religious vocation were special. Secretly I was desperate to run away from this life, to completely escape both my hometown and my family. The convent, with its strict rules, was the perfect answer to my need for a complete break with my family and everything I had suffered. I could start over, and recreate myself into a totally different person, once I left all this behind.

The next step was to get myself enrolled in a convent. I turned for help to my friend, Peggy, who had a sister in the convent. Her sister was on a mission in a small community not far from where I lived, so Peggy drove me to the convent where we met with her sister. She asked me why I believed I had a vocation. I repeated the same reasoning as I had told the priest, but I didn't tell her that I had no other options; I didn't realize it myself at that point. She told me she would ensure that the Franciscans would send me the paperwork. She also asked me to visit the Motherhouse and talk to the postulant mistress who would tell me all I needed to know. I went with Peggy that next week and met with the Sisters who answered the door. I must have said the right things because they gave me all the paperwork for embarking on my new life: get a physical; fill out the application; order the trunk with all the clothing needed for my life as a nun; report to the Motherhouse by 3:00 pm on September 3, 1965.

The biggest hurdle of this process for me was figuring out how to get a physical. I was scared to death of doctors and had never voluntarily gone to a doctor in my entire life. I asked my friend, Marian, to go with me. We only had to walk across the street, through a small park, to the only medical clinic in town. I had walked **BY** there a hundred times but never walked **IN** there. I do remember standing in a long line that stretched out the door and down the street, with my siblings, when the polio vaccination came out. I was throwing a fit because I was so scared to get the vaccine. I know my mother wanted to kill me because I was so irrational--all we had to do was suck on a sugar cube that had the medicine in it. I did put the sugar cube in my mouth but gagged on it. This story gives you an idea of how irrational my fear of doctors was. Although my friend walked me over there, she did not come in with me. I felt it would be embarrassing for the doctor and nurse to know how scared I was, so she went back to the park to wait for me.

My hand was shaking as I wrote on the questionnaire. I couldn't focus or comprehend what the questions were. The doctor asked me the same questions over and over as I tried to answer. He asked me why I needed a physical. Never good at lying, I told him that I was planning to enter the convent. It was the first time I had said it out loud to anyone other than my friend Marian. He didn't seem to be too shocked. He commented: "It is such a blessing to have the gift of a vocation in your family. I'll bet your Mom must be so proud of you." (The truth was that I hadn't even told my Mom of my plan.) I had to get into a hospital gown, me who had never taken off my clothes in front of anyone before. He listened to my heartbeat, took my blood pressure, felt my glands and peered down my throat. I worried that he might inform me I had tuberculosis or something even more dreadful. What if I didn't pass the physical? What would I do with my life if my *one and only plan* didn't work? Fear gripped me. I was eighteen years old but I was as insecure as a small child. He finally signed the paperwork, attesting to my physical fitness and soundness of mind to make this decision.

Informing Mom of my plan was a conversation that I put off as long as possible. I had made the decision six months ago but didn't want to tell her. I just wanted to keep it close to my heart for as long as I could. But Mom was becoming more and more frantic. I finally told her that I had a plan. She was visibly relieved. Then I told her that I planned to enter the Franciscan Order in September. I told her that I already had signed up and been accepted. My Mother had never supported a single decision I had made, and this was no exception.

She let loose with one of her worst tirades ever: Did I know that these "caring pillars of love" treated some kids so badly? "You know how badly you have been treated by the nuns. They profess to love everyone yet they play favorites. They give so much attention to the rich kids and ignore or abuse the poor kids." Did I plan to be part of a life that was truly a farce? Did I know that the nuns lived a lie? They took vows of poverty, but they ate better and lived better than us without any real concerns. They never went hungry. They always had the best. They did not know real poverty. If I really wanted to take a vow of poverty, I should stay right where I was because I WAS living the life of poverty.

I knew she wouldn't be happy, but I was surprised at her anger. After all, she was the die-hard Catholic who never missed a Sunday mass, said the rosary daily and read out of her Catholic missal every morning and night. She constantly prayed that God would save her. She had required all of us to take part in all her rituals, yet she violently opposed my spending my life praying as she had taught us. My only thought at that moment was: this is exactly why I want to go away and never come back.

So, my life finally had some direction. I felt relief to know that I would soon escape this small town. I started to withdraw a bit more from both my friends and my activities. I found myself wanting to work instead of going to dances. I used the excuse that I had to work, but the truth was dancing and dating seemed meaningless activities now that I was planning to leave this secular world behind.

I made one exception to this dating rule. His name was Francis. I decided to "go steady" with Francis that summer. It felt safe for me to be with him. Yes, we would neck on country roads, but as soon as he got more serious I asked him to take me home. He was always respectful of me, and we had many conversations about me entering the convent. He asked: "You enjoy me kissing you, and yet you are going away to a place where you will never be kissed again or go out on another date? Don't you ever want to get married or have kids?" I answered all of his questions with one pat answer: "I know you can't understand this, but I am being called to the religious life. It is too hard to explain but it's a gut feeling that this is what I am supposed to do." How could he argue with me about this? Having a religious vocation was not something that could be explained! So we dated and talked, and I felt comfort in knowing that I was going to get away from everything I had known for the past eighteen years. I was excited and fearful at the same time!

My friends planned a huge going-away party for me and a friend who was also going to the convent. It was held in a large room above The Corner Tap, where, as children, we had performed every year at the St. Patrick's Day celebration. The party was set for a Friday night the week before I was scheduled to leave for the convent. My friends asked if I wanted "one last date" with a guy that I had been crazy about all during high school. They would make the arrangements. I said "YES" even though I was going steady with Francis. I knew Francis would be so upset, but I did it anyway. It was a terrible night for me: I showed up with a guy who really didn't like me and my steady boyfriend was driving around all night, trying to sort out why I would do such a thing to him.

My friends went with me to shop for a dress for the party. I had decided to use some of my money to buy a dress, instead of wearing something my Mom made for me. I had few clothes because we wore uniforms from the first grade through high school. I also planned to wear this store-bought dress the day I entered the convent. I had never shopped for a dress before, so I had no idea what was in style, what size I wore, what I liked or what looked good on me. I finally chose a purple and green plaid empire-waist dress. I thought I looked as good as I could. Another friend of mine, who had decided to enter the same Franciscan Order, also bought that dress in a different color of plaid--and wore it to our going-away party.

All our friends were invited to the party. We had cake and ice cream and someone played music. Even though I loved to dance I had no fun at this last party for three reasons. I was with a guy who was with me only because my friends asked him to take me, my real boyfriend was riding around town wondering what had happened, and I did not feel comfortable being the center of attention. I couldn't wait for it to be over; the night seemed like it went on forever.

The night before I left for the convent, Francis asked me out on our last date--to Cedar Rapids for dinner and a movie. That sounded innocent enough. Francis came to pick me up. He spoke briefly to my Mom, and then we were on our way. We ate at a restaurant, and I ordered the same thing I ordered on every date I had ever had (Shrimp!). After dinner, Francis said he had decided that we should see a new movie that had just been released--*The Sound of Music*.

I had seen very few movies in my life. I had no idea what the movie was about, but it sounded interesting from what Francis told me. We had watched only a few minutes when I realized I was in big trouble. I started to cry and I couldn't stop. I had rarely cried in my life and certainly never cried with a guy. What was I going to do? I had no Kleenex. I cried and wiped my tears on my sweater all night long. I couldn't stop crying. The story hit too close to home. Maria went into a convent to escape falling in love with a man. She was a lively, beautiful girl who loved life. The mother superior realized why she had come to the convent, and she sent her away to deal with being in love with a man. I cried because I realized that I wanted to be like Maria, but I would not be sent home because I had come to the convent for the wrong reason. I had, in a sense, received my vocation and nobody was going to save me from that fate.

September 3, 1965, arrived bright and sunny. This was the day I would enter the Franciscan Order of the Holy Family of Jesus, Mary and Joseph. It was a typical beautiful fall day in Iowa. The leaves were saying goodbye to their beautiful green, giving way to the next coat of equally beautiful yellows, reds and oranges. I, too, was saying goodbye to what was. I hoped my transition would be as easy as the leaves changing color. It was wishful thinking. The next morning, Francis came to say goodbye. I walked Francis to his car. He gave me a kiss and a present, a beautiful white pearl rosary. My brothers and sisters went to school as normal. I don't even remember them saying goodbye. Two nights before, I had given away everything that I owned. Most of my clothes stayed right in the closet because my younger sister would inherit them. My only piece of jewelry, my great aunt's black onyx ring, I gave to my favorite cousin, Eileen. I used the couple of hundred dollars inherited from my grandparents to buy my convent trunk. I withdrew all the money I had saved since I started working and gave it to my Mom. I asked her to buy a new washer and dryer. I knew she would miss me the most on Saturday when I did the washing and ironing. Mom and I ate lunch together and then got in the car. Mom was quiet. What was there to say? I knew how much she didn't want me to do this. She was alone in her pain that day.

We drove the twenty-five miles to Dubuque. About halfway there we stopped to say goodbye to a friend. He was planning to enter the seminary the next week and perhaps knew better than anyone else what I was doing. We got to the Motherhouse about 2:30 pm. I was assigned the number "1442." (I was the forty-second woman to enter the convent that day. There would be forty-eight before the day was done.) As mother completed some paperwork, I was led away to a bathroom--to take off everything and replace my bra, panties, slip, nylons and dress with the simple black garb of the postulant (black tights, blouse, and skirt, a big cloth bra and white bloomer panties). I was instructed to fold up all my possessions into a neat pile, and then I walked down the long corridor to hand them to my mother and say one last goodbye. I did all this without any emotion; my Mom was equally emotionally distant. After I said goodbye I was escorted into a large room that would be our recreational area. Many of the girls were still crying. I just sat there wondering what I had gotten myself into. It did not take long to find out that this life was going to be very different from what I had imagined.

After everyone had arrived, we all introduced ourselves and shared a little bit about ourselves, including our home parish. Most had come to this life as a result of a sister who had influenced them. We proceeded to the chapel for Vespers (evening prayers) and then, the dining room for dinner. The dinner was good. I was not choosy about what I ate; I was just happy to have food. After dinner we had our first meeting. This is the moment when I started to find out what I had signed up to do. We were told what our new life would look like: Yes, we would be up at 5:00 am to meditate. We would go to chapel at 6:00 am for Mass. Breakfast at 7:00 am, then chores. College classes would begin after our chores, then more chores from 3:00 to 4:00 pm and a period for recreation from 4:00 to 5:00 pm. After Vespers in the chapel, we would go downstairs to dinner. We had a small dining room right off the main dining room. The main dining room was filled with many sisters all dressed in their habits. We sat quietly eating while we listened to a sister at the lectern reading from scripture. After that we were free to talk to our new friends.

After dinner that first night, we all went into the common recreation room where we found out our bedroom assignments. (They were called "cells".) There were five other women in my room, the "J" room (all of our names began with "J"). Each had a white curtain that pulled around her small space. In my space, I had a single bed, a small wooden dresser with all the clothes from my trunk, and a pitcher and bowl. Group recreation was from 7:00 to 8:00 pm; no talking was allowed after 8:00. Should we pass someone in the hallway, we were to look down and say: "Praised be Jesus Christ." The other person would respond "Now and forever, Amen." There must be NO talking in our bedrooms, ever! Most of us were eighteen years old.

It was hard to conceive that we could possibly honor these rules, but no one ever questioned them. It was just the way it was, and we had all signed up for this. Suffering, denial and sacrifice would win us favor with God. We were also informed that it would be a good idea to spend time with the Lord in the chapel before bed. We learned that we would not be receiving any phone calls, but we would have a chance once a week, on Saturday afternoon, to write to our families. We could receive mail every day during our recreation period, but every letter we received would be opened and read. Our first visiting day was at the end of our first year, when we received our postulant veils. We would not go home for three years. We would not leave the grounds of the Motherhouse except to see the dentist or doctor. We would not watch TV or listen to the news.

To be truthful this routine looked pretty good to me; I was used to a disciplined life. The most exciting thing for me was that I no longer had to worry about my Mom's depression, not having enough money or food, the car breaking down, not fitting in with my family, or not belonging to the "in" clique at my high school. I thought I could create my own cool clique in the convent. When I told my classmates how much I was enjoying this new life, most looked at me like I was crazy. They were crying, missing their families, and missing the lives they had left behind. I, on the other hand, felt like this was the best life I had experienced so far. I was on a new, exciting adventure, and it all looked so much better than the life I had left behind.

One of the things that made me the happiest was that I was going to be able to attend college, but I was concerned that I wouldn't be able to make it in college. I asked the nuns what would happen if someone wasn't smart enough to pass the college classes; they said that person would have to become a *cook*. In this teaching order everyone became a teacher. They said there would be special classes for those needing extra help. I knew right away that I would be one of those taking remedial classes while most of my classmates studied Shakespeare. I envied those kids, reading the classics and putting on plays. I learned that my older sister, who was attending college a few miles from the Motherhouse, had the lead in *Much Ado About Nothing*. She was starring as Beatrice, and I was studying remedial reading. It didn't seem fair, but I was so thankful to have the opportunity to study. But first, I had to learn how to study. Determined to become a good reader and make it through college, I studied all the time. Every free period found me in the library studying. I read things out loud. I kept reading things over and over until I understood them. Sometimes I never did understand, but I did not give up. After a rough start my first semester, I did better every semester after that.

The class that I remember most vividly was Music Appreciation. The sister who taught this class was the best, setting high expectations for every one of us. She was determined that we would be able to recognize the music of all the great composers. Standing by her old record player and a pile of black records, she set the needle on any part of the record, asking us to identify the work and the composer. Some of the postulants in our class, who had taken music lessons growing up, invented words to help us remember the themes. This helped all of us do better in that class.

We had a large institutional bathroom, with lots of toilets; it was right across from our bedroom and it was warm. The showers were in another room; we signed up for a time to take showers. We used a pitcher and washbasin in our rooms to wash up daily, but we could take a shower once a week. The shower room had very little light. There were no mirrors to see how you looked. I wondered how we would take care of our periods, but that was handled like everything else: very matter of factly.

Those first nine months passed by so quickly; our routine kept us very busy. Every Saturday we spent the afternoon writing letters to our families. My letters to my Mom were long and detailed. I heard nothing from the outside world so all I could relate in these letters was my daily convent life. I spent hours recounting all I learned about the Catholic Church. My family evidently thought I was becoming brainwashed. My older sister was so upset by my letters that she started regularly leaving books, magazines and newspapers for me to read on the doorsteps of the main entrance to the Motherhouse. I never saw any of these materials and only found out about them when I saw a thesaurus in the library with my sister's name in it. My postulant mistress told me that my sister had dropped it off for me to use. Since we were in training to take a vow of poverty and everything was owned communally, it was put in the library for everyone's use.

During this period some of our classmates decided that this life was not for them. Others were asked to leave. When someone decided to leave, they were not allowed to tell anyone. They simply disappeared. Whenever we noticed that someone was gone, we ran upstairs to the attic to see if we might be able to watch our friends leaving down the driveway, but we never saw them. Were they shuttled away in the middle of the night or when we were all in the chapel praying? The mistress made an announcement that so and so had decided that the religious life was not for her. It was so hard, not getting to say goodbye to our good friends. One day they were there and the next day they were gone. During my first year in the convent, I did not once question whether this was the best decision for me or if I could do this for the rest of my life, even though some of my good friends had left.

The first year, we were called "postulants." We wore black mid-calf woolen skirts, a black polyester blouse, black tights and black shoes with granny heels. Our schedule consisted of attending classes, recreation, praying and doing our chores. Our college classes were held in classrooms on the second floor of the Motherhouse. We had lots of different types of chores; these included dusting, vacuuming, and scrubbing floors, working in the laundry room, and helping in the kitchen to prepare food or set up the dining room or do dishes afterwards. After nine months of this schedule, we were part of a ceremony to receive our postulant veils--our first step in a long, eight-year process of committing to the religious life. We wrote the ceremony that spoke to the symbolism of getting our veils. During the ceremony we each received a small black nylon veil that covered our heads. The veil had a stiff white band; bobby pins were used to hold the veil in place. It was just large enough to cover our heads. The main purpose was to get us used to wearing something on our heads. It certainly made us look "nunlier"! I was definitely ready for this first step in the process.

During this time I was still receiving letters from my boyfriend, Francis. All of our mail was opened and read by the postulant mistress. After a couple of months of letters from him, I was called in by the postulant mistress and told that I could no longer receive letters from him. I was ordered to write and tell him that he should no longer write to me. I was not to mention that the nuns made me write the letter. I did as instructed, writing: "I am committing my life to Christ and I can no longer have the distractions of the worldly life, so please stop writing me. I have given up the ways of the world. Please no longer send any correspondence to me." That was the end of that part of my life. I later heard that Francis signed up with the Navy for seven years on the day he got my letter. That sounded drastic but then I realized that I had signed up for the convent for the rest of my life. Seven years didn't sound so bad!

The nuns also read every letter that was mailed out of the convent. Every letter we wrote was left unsealed on the mistress's desk. We did figure out a way to get around this rule. On visiting day we could send mail out with our families. But there would be no visiting day for a whole year. By then it really didn't matter. We were totally indoctrinated into convent thinking and the rigid way of life that would put us in good favor with God and save our souls from eternal damnation (hell).

Were we ever allowed to leave the Mount? Yes and no but mostly NO! We did take the bus to visit the doctor and the dentist. I had some cavities and made a number of visits to the dentist who turned out to be our postulant mistress's brother. We always went on these trips with at least one or two other postulants. These trips were scary because, having been locked up for more than six months, we felt uncomfortable being out in public. People stared at us and talked about us.

What was the hardest thing about being in the convent? Music depravation! During high school I had LOVED music and dancing. I grew up listening to the radio that sat on top of the refrigerator. I actually danced with the refrigerator to the music coming from the radio. So when I realized that I would never again hear any rock and roll music, my heart was heavy, all the joy taken from my soul.

Like a number of my classmates, I had smoked some during high school but never could get the knack of inhaling. Truthfully, I didn't really want to learn because I had heard how bad it was for your lungs. In our first days at the Motherhouse, a couple of the girls actually picked up butts discarded by local hired hands, and smoked them. I had the good fortune to be in the same dormitory with Jeanie, who had smoked a lot in high school. One day she received a package in the mail. (The rule about receiving packages was that the food must be put in the recreation room for everyone to share.) Her package contained a whole box of fudge, the best fudge I had ever tasted. She snuck it up to her room, and for at least a week we sneaked into her "cell" to eat the fudge. With no utensils we just grabbed huge chunks of it with our fingers. It was so much fun to eat.

The biggest bonus, however, was hidden deep in the box. To this day I am not sure how that package passed inspection. When Jeanie discovered the cigarettes, we immediately began plotting how we would sneak away to smoke them. There were four of us in this adventure. Surely if we went far enough away from the Motherhouse into the fields, no one would ever know what we were up to? We swore each other to secrecy, but could we trust each other? This was a big risk for us because if even one person cheated, we would all be in serious trouble. The day finally arrived. We met out by the Stations of the Cross. We hoped we would look like we were going for an innocent walk. We didn't all leave together. When we all four met up we were so excited. We walked quickly. When we felt that we were far enough away from the building, we lit up our Marlboros. I tried to inhale. It didn't work but I was so happy to be part of this group. At least that is what I thought at that moment.

After smoking a couple of cigarettes, it was time to head back to the convent. It was at that point that I freaked out. What if the nuns could smell the smoke? What if they had noticed we were missing? What would happen to us if we did get caught? My mind began to race. I was sure that God would punish me for such a blatant violation of the rules. I was always the good girl. I couldn't even think about getting kicked out of the convent. Why had I taken this risk? Was I addicted to nicotine? I vowed I would NEVER again put myself at risk for this kind of trouble. I went straight to my room and brushed my teeth, then joined the rest of our class as they were going into chapel. They wanted to know where we were. Our response: we just said we had taken too long of a walk and lost track of time. I never found out if the other girls finished that package of cigarettes, but I was never again a part of it.

It was Christmas time and some of us were longing to watch TV. One of the girls found out that *White Christmas* was on that night. We were not allowed to watch it, but we all knew there was a TV in the basement. After we had our recreation, we were supposed to go to chapel, say our night prayers and then head upstairs to our bedrooms. That would be close to 8:00, the time when we were only allowed to say: "Praised be Jesus Christ." The word spread that we were going to sneak down to the basement to watch *White Christmas*. We knew we would be in serious trouble if we got caught, but we were willing to take the chance. We plugged in the TV, found the channel, and settled in on some wooden chairs we found at the other end of the basement. The movie was just getting good when the postulant mistress surprised us, stood in front of the TV with her arms crossed and very sternly demanded we return upstairs where we were supposed to be!

You can be sure we got quite a lecture that next morning! We learned very quickly that the pain inflicted was not worth the price of disobeying the rules. Since we went to confession every Saturday, we would have to confess. Actually, I was relieved to have something to confess. It was so hard coming up with something new to say every week. I stood in line outside the Confessional, waiting for the priest to hear my confession, in anguish over what I would say. I usually confessed that I had been unkind to a friend or had disobeyed the mistress or had taken something that didn't belong to me. I repeated these "sins" week after week for years, even though I had not committed any such sins.

During recreation, in winter time, we went tobogganing and skating. Both activities were great fun, but we didn't have the clothes to keep warm in the cold Iowa winters. We needed heavier mittens, scarves and boots to venture outside in the below zero weather. Pants were out of the question, so our legs got very cold. We must have looked frightful (and cold!) in our habits, climbing onto the toboggans for a ride down the hills near the Motherhouse. Skating was also cold but somewhat more manageable garbed in our habits.

I had been in the convent about ten months when the postulant mistress called me into her office. As I waited I wondered if she found out that I had been smoking. Was she going to ask me to leave? My mind was running wild. My worst fear was about to be realized. She came in, closed the door and announced: "Your Mother has had a heart attack. We think it is important for you to visit her in the hospital. I have arranged for your parish priest to take you to the town where your Mother is hospitalized." My first reaction was to ask myself: "Do I really have to go see her?" I was so scared to see Mom. I hadn't seen or talked to her in ten months; I hadn't seen any of my family. None of us had left the Motherhouse at all except for doctor visits. We had not yet even had our first visiting day. Everyone was envious that I was getting to leave for an overnight. I was scared. The priest picked me up, and we went straight to the hospital. He planned to visit with me and my Mom and then take me to a local convent. This convent belonged to the same Order of St. Francis that I was in. After Mass he would come for me, take me for another short visit to the hospital and then return me to the Motherhouse.

I remember being shocked to see my mother looking so frail. She was in intensive care, hooked up to all sorts of tubes. I didn't know what to say. I really didn't have to say anything because she was too sick. It had been almost a year since I had spoken to her. The priest filled up the empty spaces of conversation. I remember him saying that she had better get well quickly because she had a younger daughter who was "being wild and running the streets". "You know, Helen, it is not going to be good to leave that daughter alone for any length of time." It was a sobering experience for me because I had all but forgotten about my brothers and sisters who were still dealing with the life I had so gladly left behind. I just wanted to leave and go back to the convent; this was too uncomfortable for me to deal with. On the way back, I didn't say a word.

Upon returning to the convent I found a situation that I could never have imagined. Everyone in my class had gotten chiggers, the result of a long hike! Everyone was itching, out of control. I was the only one without chiggers; I felt alone and lost and left out. They were all jealous of me getting to see my family. They were suffering from the constant itching. Nothing else mattered at the time. I wanted to tell them how painful it was for me to see my mother in the hospital hooked up to all the tubes.

Our first summer in the convent presented some problems for me and my classmates, especially adjusting to wearing those long black dresses with black tights and black granny shoes all summer long. Gone were the shorts and tops and sandals of the past summers. It was hot and humid all summer long and it rained a lot. That year, the Mississippi River was flooding. We could only imagine the destruction below as the river overran its banks. We were all safe, out of harm's way, because the convent was located on a huge cliff overlooking the Mississippi.

One day during recreation time, several of us went up to the attic where the elderly nuns' trunks were stored. It was a rainy day and there was nothing interesting to do, so we started exploring some of the old trunks. Somehow the postulant mistress got wind of our activity. She immediately assembled the entire class and sternly informed us that she knew we were doing things we shouldn't be doing. She required each of us to make an individual confession to her in her office of all our wrongdoings. She said we should include in our confession *everything* that we were doing that was wrong.

We were called to her office one at a time. We were not allowed to talk to each other so we couldn't compare notes. As I waited in line, I saw my friend come out. She rolled her eyes and looked down. I wondered if she had confessed to the smoking or the food in our rooms. No, I decided, I would not bring up anything except the most recent incident. I admitted that I was in the attic but I, personally, had not taken anything out of the trunks. (Some of my classmates, however, had been fooling around and dressing up with things they found in the trunks.) She told me that I was guilty by association, that I had no right to look in anyone else's trunk. She ended by asking me to personally assess whether this religious life was for me. (Later we found out that she asked this question to every one of our classmates!)

The summer went by quickly because we had not only attended summer school but also had lots of work in the garden. The garden was huge and located in back of the Motherhouse. Working in the garden was part of our chore assignment. Our first visiting day finally arrived. I was so worried because my Mom was still quite weak from her heart attack; she might not be able to come. Everyone was very excited to see their families but I was worried. First, I didn't know if my family would even come. If they did come, what kind of shape would my mother be in? I felt so distant from my brothers and sisters. What would I say to them? I felt my family was different from the other families.

Well, the day did turn out okay. Mom arrived with my siblings. We took pictures and talked about general things. My sister declared that I had been brainwashed. My siblings were all distant. It was clear they thought I was crazy to be living this life, and this one day confirmed their suspicions. They could no longer relate to anything I was saying or doing.

My postulant year was now coming to an end. Did I ever look back and say that I needed to get out of there? Never! Not once did I question my decision to enter the convent. I did feel there was no turning back. It had been a year of clean sheets, good food, warm nights and new friends, and I was working on getting closer to God. Where was God? How could I get in touch with Him? If I prayed hard enough, would I eventually get to know Him? I had been taught that if I sacrificed everything for Him, I would be rewarded with a close personal relationship with God.

One of the activities aimed at helping us get closer to God was a ten-day retreat at the end of our postulant year. I was appalled when I heard that we were required to remain silent for the entire TEN days! I had no idea how I was going to do this. I loved to talk to my friends. How could I go ten days without talking to anyone? I feared this would push me over the edge. I just didn't have the tools to entertain myself for ten straight days. At the end of this retreat, we would become canonicals and begin our second year of convent life. I somehow made it through the ten days and moved into the new stage of my convent life.

I started to ponder which names I should submit to the Mother Superior. She would make the final decision, but I could submit three requests for the Sister name I wanted. I first requested Sister Vincent, after my Dad. My second request was Sister Tara. My third was Sister Sara Marie. I predicted they would choose Sister Vincent because there was a sentimental reason for that name. Sister Tara sounded too much like "Sister Terror." I chose Sister Sara Marie because I loved the name Sara, and Marie was my middle name.

In the vows ceremony we would become brides of Jesus Christ. The postulant mistress asked us to meet her on the third floor of the convent. She took us to a room that had always been locked. It was filled with a rack of old faded wedding dresses. I tried on a few but none seemed to fit me well. Finally, one of my classmates handed me a dress that was too small for her. It fit me, but I sure didn't feel like a beautiful bride. I didn't really know what it should feel like to be a bride of Christ, or any kind of bride, for that matter. Maybe it was because I was wearing black granny shoes under the bride's gown? I would also be carrying something strange: instead of flowers, a brown habit (the only clothing I would have for the rest of my life). I would take the vows of poverty, chastity and obedience. Even though I would take these temporary vows for three years in a row, I had to treat them as if they were, in my mind, final vows. After I took final vows, I would have to petition the Pope if I ever wanted to leave the convent.

The day of the ceremony was a hot, sunny, humid Midwestern day. My family and friends arrived. We were lined up one by one in our bridal gowns. The large chapel was packed with our invited guests. I did not look for my friends or family as we marched, single file, down the center aisle carrying the brown Franciscan habit. It felt strange to be dressed in white and carrying a heavy brown habit. I would go in as Janice McDermott and come out of the chapel with a different name. During the vows ceremony I learned the Mother Superior had chosen Sister Sara Marie for me.

During the ceremony we left carrying our habits and came back dressed in our habits. My habit consisted of a long flowing brown dress with a scapula (a long flowing piece of material with a hole in the middle to put my head through) that covered my entire body, both front and back over my dress. My dress had three-quarter length sleeves; under the sleeves was a see-through black sleeve that had elastic on one end to hold it up under the sleeves. The idea was to cover the entire arm. I wore a white veil that covered my head except for my bangs, a large, heavy black rosary around my waist, and a medium-sized cross around my neck. We would get a ring to wear on our left ring finger when we took final vows.

So my life as a novice began. This second year was more intense. It was a year of strictly religious study; we did not take any college classes. Only in our third year were we allowed to read any secular newspapers, books, or magazines or to watch TV. My sister continued to be upset about how I had been cut off from the world, so she brought me more things to read. Although she had not seen me, she could tell from the tone of my letters that I was becoming more steeped in the deeply-held doctrine of the Catholic Church.

Shortly after we became novices a new group of postulants arrived at the Motherhouse. They immediately informed us that we were totally "brainwashed". One member of the group was especially vocal about her concern. (It was true that we didn't know anything about what had happened over the past year.) We often snuck into the closet to listen to her stories. We closed the door and escaped into another world, listening to her play her guitar and sing Simon and Garfunkel and Beatles songs. She knew most of the songs by heart and had the most beautiful voice. She did many songs but my favorite song was *Bridge Over Troubled Waters*. We all knew she would get in trouble if she were ever caught singing outside of recreational time. She eventually did get in trouble, and as a result, her guitar was locked up except during recreation. I fondly remember those few times in the closet as some of my happiest moments in the convent.

It was during this year that I got called into the canonical mistress's office. She said she had some serious concerns about me. She said my laugh was too loud and unbecoming, that I had to be very careful of how I sat. She said that if I couldn't control my laugh and sit properly "as a sister", I would need to seriously look at whether this was the life for me. I hate to admit it but I never took that threat seriously. I continued to laugh loud. I had always been flexible and could sit cross-legged easily. (I did try to sit properly when I was around the mistress.)

Talking about sex in the convent is not easy for me. I grew up being so uncomfortable with being touched. Being in the convent was perfect for me in that respect. We were not expected or allowed to touch each other.

One night right before the eight o'clock rule of not speaking to each other, one of my fellow classmates asked to come to my room to give me a backrub. (She was the only one in our class who was studying to be a nurse.) As part of her training she was to learn the technique of massage so she was practicing on her classmates. She came to my room and started giving me a great massage. It was not long before I was totally relaxed and had an orgasm. I was very nervous and upset about this. I wondered if she knew what had happened. I decided that it was just too dangerous for her to practice on me. From that day forward I never again let her come to my room to practice her techniques. Later she said to me: "I guess you didn't like the way I gave you a massage." I didn't say anything. How could I say that I thought that her giving me an orgasm regularly would lead me down a road that was too scary and sinful for me to get involved in? We were told our bodies were sacred. We were brides of Christ. We took a vow of chastity. We would take no pleasure from our bodies. I knew it was wrong.

What I observed and experienced the next four years would open my eyes to a whole new meaning for the word: "sex". During our weekly meetings, the mistress talked to us about what she called "particular friendships". Much later in life I was able to identify the meaning of "particular friendships" as lesbian relationships. At first we didn't have a clue what she was talking about because we had never heard of "particular friendships". She was so vague in how she described these friendships. We all wondered if we had one. We were told that these friendships were a mortal sin and must stop immediately. Over time I began to notice that many of our classmates had paired up with another sister, spending a great deal of time together alone. The same thing happened to me. I had become infatuated with another sister who was a year ahead of me. I wanted to be with her all the time, to talk to her, to walk with her. She was very pretty, lively, and smart and played the guitar. I was nervous around her. I felt different around her. I worshipped the ground she walked on. I hung on her every word. Every chance I got, I would try to sit by her. I never talked to her about how I felt, so I never knew if she realized how crazy I was about her. I hardly realized what had happened to me. It was only after she left the Motherhouse at the end of my second year in the convent that I realized how deeply attached I was to her. I felt terribly alone and depressed. It was my first experience with this kind of loss. Even though I never saw or engaged in any sexual relations during my five years in the convent, we thought certain relationships might fall into the category of "particular friendships".

It was during this time that I had my first concerns about living my whole life with only women. Since there were no men around to love, might I find myself falling in love with a woman? I wondered if I was a lesbian. I found myself wishing that I had a rich, loving family that would drive up to the front of the Motherhouse and whisk me away. I wanted to cry but no tears would come. I thought: "What have I gotten myself into?"

During our canonical year we concentrated on deepening our religious life. We learned to sacrifice as much as we could to atone for our sins. One of the practices that we used to get closer to God was a posture that symbolized our surrender to God. After evening prayers we would go to the chapel and hold our arms out and up, as if we were being arrested. This posture, which was held for long periods of time, showed that we were willing to suffer for Christ and surrender to His will. We also said many prayers during these periods of arm holding. I tried to hold my arms up as long as the older sisters, who would sit in the chapel for hours. I would plead with God to come to me, to speak to me, to let me get to know Him. I was willing to give my life to Him. All I needed was a little word from Him. I was beginning to feel somewhat desperate. Other sisters advised me to persevere and I would eventually find God.

Another convent practice that was dying out by the time I entered the convent in 1965 was a "chapter of faults". We experienced this only once. We lay flat on the floor, prostrating our bodies, confessing our faults and begging for forgiveness for all our sins. We lay on the floor, side by side, for a long time as we verbally confessed our sins.

Our second year ended with another ten-day retreat, again not speaking for ten days. This one was a bit easier because we had so many books to read and passages from the bible to meditate on. We were instructed to think much more about what vows would mean to us and how we were dedicating our lives to Christ. At this time two classmates were asked to leave. We had started two years ago with forty-eight women. We were now down to forty-two classmates.

In our third year we were the oldest group at the Motherhouse, most of us just turning twenty. We resumed a full load of college courses. We went to classes, prayed, worked and studied. We had settled into a routine. Many of us had adjusted to this austere lifestyle, and when the next group of postulants arrived, we didn't have much to do with them. I remained happy that I was in this safe haven. The sacrifice of not going home, talking on the phone or seeing my friends or family rarely bothered me. In fact, most of them stopped writing me during this third year. I was still so happy to be away from my former life and to be totally consumed by this new life.

College seemed to be getting easier for me. I wanted to feel smart so I studied as much as I could. I had lots of time so it was easy to study. I was proud to be passing my college classes but was still required to take a remedial class. To my dismay, I was not allowed to take the Shakespeare course with my classmates because it was offered at the same time as the remedial reading/grammar class. My classmates were learning famous lines from Shakespeare and acting out scenes from his plays. I longed to talk to my sister about her role as Beatrice, if only I had taken the class. My classmates learned calligraphy while I attended a lab for the remedial class. I refused to get discouraged. I asked my friends to teach me to do calligraphy. I borrowed their pens and practiced right along with them.

Even though my older sister was in college a few miles away, there was no way she could contact me. But her life still impacted mine. She was getting a degree in Drama, and I guess she thought she was an expert about being a nun because she had a sister in the convent. One evening she and a friend went into the costume department and took what they needed to dress up like nuns. They proceeded to take a taxi to a local high school that was operated by my order and tried to get into the play for free, pleading that they had no money. Of course, they were caught and punished. The news made it to the Motherhouse, and I was sufficiently embarrassed.

During this third year of my life in the convent, my older sister graduated from college. This day should have been a big event in our family. She was setting the standard for all of us. She had led the way. She had endured. My father had an eighth-grade education and my Mom, a high school education. No one else could have realized how much this accomplishment meant to our family, but it was out of the question for me to even think about attending her graduation.

Shortly after she graduated from college, she got married to a man who was a mechanical engineer. He had taken a job in Los Angeles with Martin Marietta. My sister planned to join him after the wedding. The wedding was only a few miles from the Motherhouse, but I was not allowed to attend. My younger sister was her maid of honor. They were permitted to visit me after the reception so I could meet my new brother-in-law and see my sister. I waited all day for them to come. It got dark. I waited and waited and finally, I got a call to come to the front parlor. There I saw my sister, dressed in a beautiful wedding gown with a mink collar. Her long beautiful hair was pulled up into a French bun. My other sister and my cousin looked just as beautiful. My mother looked exhausted and overwhelmed; she surely missed having her husband there to give away her oldest daughter. I am not sure if she found any consolation in her daughter marrying a kind, loving man from a good family who would give her daughter the life she was programmed to want.

I was shaken for a few days after this event. It brought home to me so vividly how removed I was from my family. I hadn't even known my sister had a serious boyfriend or any of the details of the wedding.

My family's life was moving forward, but I had no part in it. My brother had graduated from high school and entered the Air Force. That left only two siblings at home to carry the responsibility of taking care of my Mom. Only two siblings receiving Aid to Families with Dependent Children meant less and less money for my Mom. How was she making it? I, however, had only momentary concerns about my family. I continued to feel happy that I no longer had to worry about my Mom's mental or physical health.

There was another concern that started to bother me during this third year. If I was supposed to become the bride of Christ, why were there no signs that God was pleased with my dedication? Could I dedicate my whole life to something or someone so silent? Feeling that I needed some signs that God was pleased, I prayed and prayed and prayed for any sign. I got nothing. When I asked my classmates about this, they said that is where faith and trust entered the picture. I just needed to trust that God would be there for me and that I was his beloved child with whom He was well pleased. I was not yet questioning whether I should do this. I was sure it was the right decision.

Life continued outside the convent. The Beatles were recording new songs. John Glenn had landed on the moon. Momentous events were exploding around us but we were oblivious to most of these events. The world was going on but we were frozen in time. We were busy focusing on learning how to pray and dedicating our lives to God. I did not give a thought to life outside the walls of the Motherhouse. We were totally isolated and that was fine with me. We did hear news of an event that would affect us greatly. The Vatican Council was meeting in Rome. Pope John XXIII was suggesting sweeping changes for the Catholic Church--changes that would move it into modern times. As part of these "sweeping changes" we were given permission to go back to our secular names. So, instead of Sister Sara Marie, I could be called Sister Janice. We also were given the choice of making either vows or promises. I chose to return to Sister Janice and I decided to take vows. Things became more unsettled as each of my classmates tried to decide what they wanted to do. We were confused. We had signed up for a specific life but now all of that was drastically changing. The changes were for the better, but they did create a lot of uncertainty.

I had now lived in an institution for three years, and I started to wonder what it would be like to go home for the first time in three years. Who would I see? Would people look at me funny? How would my family react to me? I had seen them only twice in the past three years. Would my friends come to see me? What would I say to them? What would I say to my family? Would they be able to attend the vows ceremony?

My Mom continued to struggle with her health. During this third year she had another heart attack. I was not allowed to visit her this time. I wondered if she would be strong enough to attend my vows ceremony. After the ceremony, I would be permitted to stay with my family for five days and then travel across the state on a train with my classmates to finish my last two years of school. Immediately after graduation, I would be assigned to a mission. The next couple of years were well scripted.

As we were preparing for the ceremony, one of my closest friends disappeared from the convent. The skill of the nuns in sneaking our classmates out of the Motherhouse always amazed us. She, of course, was not allowed to say goodbye. I am sure she was sworn to secrecy about her plan to leave. The other possibility was that, once the decision to leave had been made, that person was immediately shipped off. She never told a single person she was leaving. She was just gone. I was so sad because I wasn't sure if I would ever see her again. (She was the friend who was so much fun, who gave me the fudge, the brownies and the cigarettes.) I was sure she had decided that smoking, dating and having a good time with her friends was too much to give up. She was from a wealthy family who could just drive up in their mobile home and take her away.

The day of my vows dawned sunny, very hot and humid. It was August 10th, 1968. A number of extended family members had also been invited. Dad's brother, Uncle Cyril, would represent his side of the family. My aunt and uncle came from Chicago. My siblings were there. Mom did come but she was weak and tired. My Uncle Walter, who had taken care of my smallest brother for a year while we were in the orphanage, was there. He was very talkative and so excited to be part of this "magnificent ceremony". I got the feeling that he was much more excited about the ceremony than he was interested in his niece who had just taken vows. The day passed quickly. There were so many visitors. Forty-eight of us had entered three years ago; now thirty-four of us had taken our first vows. We all left with our families at the end of this day--to make our first home visit in three years. We also said goodbye to the Motherhouse. It was an emotional time for all of us. We had grown and changed, but lots more changes were to come. I was twenty-one.

My first visit home after three years was a shock. I can't describe it any other way. I knew I had grown even more distant from my family, but this visit confirmed the gulf that had widened between us. I had seen my family once a year for the past three years and written to them weekly, but their lives had gone in a completely different direction. I realized I had nothing to say to them. I felt so uncomfortable being outside the convent walls for the first time; all of life I had known the past three years was gone. It felt like I was standing on quicksand; everything was shifting. My younger brother was in the Air Force; my younger sister was living with an aunt and uncle while attending beauty school; my older sister was married and living in California. My youngest brother was the only sibling at home, attending the Catholic high school. He was very bright and asking too many questions in his religion classes. He had gotten into trouble with the priest during religion classes and incurred his wrath. He was not in a mood to deal with his sister's blind faith in the Catholic religion.

That left my Mom and me to interact with each other. I had imagined that things might be different between us because I had witnessed other families interacting, but she was as distant as ever. She was grieving the loss of her daughter to a system with which she deeply disagreed but had followed so faithfully for so many years. My vows had sealed my commitment to this "new life". It seemed that absence had not made the heart grow fonder.

Some of my friends did come to visit. I felt shy and embarrassed about the way I looked, and I couldn't carry on a conversation about the normal things people talk about--current events, TV shows, movies, fashions. More than anything, I was overwhelmed by how small the house felt. I had been living in an institution and now my house felt like a miniature doll house. When the week was over, I was more than happy to board the train and head west to the opposite end of the state to finish my junior and senior years at Briar Cliff College, a private Catholic college. My Mom drove me to the southern part of Iowa, about 100 miles away, to catch the train.

I was so excited to get on the train. I was embarking on a new adventure! Soon we would learn that we would have a lot more freedom. Here we would be in class with students our age, even males, because the campus had become co-ed the year before.

Most of my classmates were already on the train. Others came on board as the train passed their towns. They all talked about how their home visits went. I didn't say a word. We spoke to some of the passengers on the train about being Catholic. They said they weren't Catholic, but were Methodist or Lutheran. I thought to myself: "I wonder if they know they are going to hell?" I was beginning to question this whole idea: How could a loving God send so many people to hell simply because they didn't belong to the Catholic Church?

The trip was wonderful. I loved every moment of the click clacking of the steel wheels hitting the rails. Every mile was taking me to a new adventure and farther away from the life I had known in eastern Iowa. I had never even been to western Iowa. In fact, I had only gone about 90 miles from my home in one direction. I remember seeing my first Black person on the train that day. I tried not to stare. I never closed my eyes during this trip. I was twenty-two years old, beginning my fourth year in the convent and moving clear across the state. I loved a new adventure and this was one.

We arrived at our station at 10:30 pm and were picked up by two young sisters who came in uniforms that looked more relaxed than anything we had seen at the Motherhouse. They wore veils but not the long, heavy kind. They were talking to us as if they didn't have to observe that rule of silence. After all, it was 10:30 at night! It was two and half hours after they were to be silent. They assured us that life would be very different for us at the "Cliff". We were quickly shown to our rooms. We each carried one black suitcase; our trunks would arrive later, with all of our earthly possessions.

I was very excited to see one of our convent classmates, one of those who had "disappeared" in the middle of the night. Her family lived nearby and we had already heard that she was attending our college. (She was my friend with the illicit cigarettes.) I was so excited to see her! She came right over and offered to take me to dinner, accompanied by her boyfriend. It made me feel even more self-conscious. How had she changed so dramatically? When I saw her I began to wonder what it would be like--to wear regular clothes, apply makeup, smell so good and have a boyfriend. We had little to say to each other. She announced that she was getting married soon and wanted to know if I would be in her wedding! She would sneak me out of the convent, buy me a bridesmaid's dress; she would pay for everything. How I laughed. There was no way I could ever do that. I would be breaking all the rules! It was too far out of my comfort zone to even imagine how I would look in anything but black.

Life, indeed, was very different from the Motherhouse. The first thing we discovered, to our delight, was we would each have our very own room!!!! Each room sported a single bed, a small area for a sink and toilet and a desk with a shelf above it for our books. It was actually possible to go to our room and close the door. We did share a large institutional bathroom. The large building, which was shared with the priest, was multipurpose. We were on the second and third floors, and the priest's quarters, on the first floor.

The large reception area near the entrance was used by the students. One late afternoon I was surprised to stumble upon a party there for women in the dorms to introduce them to a line of the finest china patterns, the options for flatware and a luxurious line of pots and pans. I was fascinated by this so I stopped to watch. This was so foreign to my world; never had I dreamed of owning such items. I watched them ordering so many necessities for their married life, a life I would never have. Several girls from my classes invited me to come over and join them but I told them I needed to study. I went to my room and sat there for the longest time, realizing that this was a whole new world I just observed. When I was growing up we had inherited old pots, pans and dishes from our Great Aunts Winnie and Gertie. We did have good dishes and good silverware that we used on special occasions, but I never thought about picking out my own patterns.

At the Cliff, we were bombarded with so many new things we had never experienced at the Motherhouse. Each floor had a TV, where we could watch the news or other educational programs. The older sisters who taught at the college were sharing these two floors with us, so they were the ones who decided what we watched. I spent very little time there since I didn't like TV and did not feel comfortable socializing with the older sisters. I started to wonder how I would survive when I was on a mission with mostly older sisters.

Classes began shortly after we arrived. I jumped full speed into my studies. I wanted to make sure I stayed on top of my classes. I studied endlessly in my room. As a result of a lifetime of lacking confidence, I continued to worry that I would fail a class. Everything here seemed harder to me. There were so many more students in our classes, and they all seemed smarter than me. I put so much pressure on myself to succeed. I was a nun; I HAD to do well.

Very soon, I was faced with the decision to declare a major. The truth was that I never thought I would ever graduate from college because I didn't think I was smart enough. Now I had to plan for the last two years, taking courses in my major. I didn't feel like I could "major" in anything. I had no confidence that I could be a teacher, but I had joined a teaching order. Might they ask me to leave if I told them I didn't want to teach? I knew I was required to teach but felt that social work would be something that suited me better. I did feel quite strongly about the way my family had been treated during those years that social workers were regular visitors at our home. I had even stronger emotions about how we had been treated by our teachers when I was a child. I wanted to be the kind of teacher/social worker that my family desperately needed those years we were in crisis. So I made the decision to major in Sociology with a minor in Education. The college did not yet offer a major in Education.

My sociology classes were the most interesting of all my courses. It was 1969. In one course, we discussed the future of the leisure class and how so many labor-saving devices would ensure the freedom to relax and have fun. We were asked to fantasize about what we would do with all of our leisure time.

The best part about majoring in sociology: we were all required to do field placements. My first placement was at the Indian Center downtown. We went into Indian family homes to help them with whatever they needed. I vividly remember washing an aging woman's hair. We also did housecleaning, errands and other chores. It also provided me an opportunity to better interact with some of my classmates. Some of their questions were disturbing to me: "You don't seem like the nun type. Why did you go to the convent? Are you happy there? It doesn't seem like you are happy. You laugh so funny; you seem like you are having a good time. Are you sure this is what you really want to do? Have you ever thought about leaving the convent?" I didn't really have good answers to these questions. No, I had never thought about leaving but I could not explain why. They would not understand the way of life I had learned: once you have made a decision, you act on it without questioning it. "You made your bed; now lay in it" was a saying my Mom repeated regularly. My life was focused solely on living the decision I had made.

At this very same time something happened that was pivotal to determining the route my future would take. I was put in charge of preparing the chapel for Mass every morning. This entailed getting up early to lay out the chaplain's vestments, light the candles, pour the wine and open the Bible to the day's readings. One morning on the way to the sacristy, the chaplain asked if I had ever thought about leaving. I answered emphatically: "NEVER". He replied: "More than likely you will probably leave the convent." I was, of course, quite shaken by this statement. I asked him why. He said that an unexamined life is a sure sign that you will wake up at some point and decide that you want to be somewhere else. He said it was important to ask that question often. I went back to my room and asked myself the question: "Do I want to leave?" I quickly said to myself: "Of course not. You have chosen this life for many very good reasons." In any case, there was no way to turn back and I should not even entertain such a sinful thought. This was hard to reconcile because it WAS the priest who asked me to ponder this astounding question. I was confused so I decided to ignore his advice.

This year at the Cliff went very quickly. When the school year was over, our class stayed at the college for the summer, taking courses and preparing to renew our vows. It was a fun time but also a tumultuous one because a group of the young nuns who had been out on a mission, but hadn't finished college, returned to study for the summer. These young missionaries introduced us to new ways of looking at the Catholic Church. Some had embraced "speaking in tongues" and the Pentecostal Movement, and they encouraged us to speak in tongues as well. It seemed we were getting into some dangerous stuff, but it was all so exciting and interesting. The older nuns were very suspicious when they caught wind of us doing the "Pentecostal thing". They accused us of being Communists, and they became more and more hostile and suspicious. More and more of my classmates were talking about leaving.

More unsettling changes came about. We were told that we no longer had to wear habits; we could wear simple blouses and black skirts. Again we were given the choice to renew vows or take promises. I put all my doubts behind me and had decided by the end of the summer to take vows again. At the ceremony in the college chapel, all of us who were taking vows stood up one at a time to recite our vows.

I had just one visitor from my family during this year, my younger sister. She had completed beauty school and was on her way to California to live with my older sister and her husband. She was dating this really cute guy from a well-to-do family that owned a trucking company. He had driven her across the state in one of his family-owned semi-trailer trucks. She visited briefly. I arranged for her to get to the station where she would take the train to L.A. I questioned her about why she had decided to say goodbye to this cute guy with a lot of money. She explained that she had higher aspirations in life, that because she was able to make it through beauty school she believed she could also graduate from college. The truth was that being a beautician didn't suit her; she didn't like the gossip in beauty shops so she took a job working on wigs and in funeral homes.

The fall season came around quickly. Western Iowa was every bit as beautiful as eastern Iowa. The trees were dressed in the most beautiful colors of reds, oranges and yellows. Students returned to the campus. It was my senior year in college. I was now twenty-three. Getting back to classes made me nervous and excited. I was on the verge of having a dream come true. I didn't allow myself to get too excited yet because it still seemed to me an impossible dream. I just couldn't believe I was making it through college. Did anyone else know what a miracle this was?

That last year brought so many changes that it still makes my head spin to think about it all. A friend I had known since we were children came to the Cliff. We had many long talks, and one day, she said something that completely shook me up: "If I was as unhappy as you seem to be, I would do something about it." No one had ever said anything like that to me. I asked her what I should do. She suggested that I talk to the school counselor and I decided I would take her advice. I had no idea how that decision would radically change my life. I walked by the counseling office a few times before I gathered the courage to go in and make the appointment. I learned that there was only one counselor and he was a MAN. What could he possibly know about what I was going through?

I made the appointment and immediately began to feel better. I didn't know what would transpire, but at least I had hope that someone might help me sort out why I felt so unhappy. The unhappiness had sort of snuck up on me during the past year at the college. I had no way of knowing why I was so unhappy; I wasn't even able to give it a name until my friend said it.

This counselor turned out to be one of the best. I am sure he could tell how nervous it made me to talk to him. He instructed me to sit down and suggested that I take some time and relax for a few minutes. He then encouraged me to talk about my life. I told him about my growing-up years and how I had decided to go to the convent. He came to the conclusion that I was trying to decide whether I should leave the convent. I violently disagreed with him. He asked me: "Do you want to leave?" I said "No!!!!" He instructed me to think about that question and return in a week. I went back to my room and I thought about it. I thought about it. I thought about it. I went back the next week. He asked me the same question. I told him that I didn't believe I wanted to leave. He told me to go back and think about it and come back in another week. I did this again. This time I admitted to myself that I would like to leave BUT there was no way I could leave. The next week I told him just that. Again, he told me to go back and think about it for a week. That next week when I returned to his office, I admitted that I wanted to leave. He replied: "YOU CAN LEAVE."

That was all it took. He had given me permission. Right then and there, I decided I would leave the convent. I felt like a huge weight had been lifted off my shoulders. I went back to my room, and I lay on my bed for hours. In fact, every minute I had free, I lay on my bed and thought about leaving. Life seemed to be pouring back into my body. My heart was so happy. I tried to imagine what it would be like. I decided not to tell anyone. I needed to live with this decision for awhile. It was so radical for me! It went against everything I had been programmed to believe about how I would live my life. What would I do? Where would I go? How would I pull this off? I had no money, no clothes, no possessions, and no job. The first thing to do was tell my Superior. Amazingly, she seemed resigned to it. She didn't even act surprised. So many of my classmates were leaving or had left. She did ask me if I was sure of my decision. I said: "YES."

I asked her for the money to purchase a ticket to take the train across Iowa to give this news to my Mom. I was sure she would not be happy about my decision because she had never been happy about anything that I had done. In this case, however, I really underestimated my mother's reaction!

I never went back to see the counselor after I reached this decision in late November. I made my train reservation in early December. I would leave on the Friday before Christmas, spending a week at my Mom's house over Christmas break. This would be only the second time I had been home in five years. My married sister was also there visiting. I really needed her to be there because I thought she would support my decision more than anyone else; she had been the most vocal in opposing my decision to go into the convent. I was counting on her to help me get me out of the convent.

That train trip was actually quite eventful. It was 1969 and one of the coldest, snowiest winters on record in Iowa. After I boarded the train in Sioux City, it wasn't long before word started circulating that the train might not make it to its destination because of the snow and severe cold. The windows of the train were completely frozen. It was cold inside the train. I wondered if someone from my family would be able to come for me. Even though we were several hours late, we finally arrived and my family did meet the train.

I have no memory of that Christmas, what gifts I got or even if I gave anyone a gift. I do remember telling my sister I needed to talk to her-- alone. There was still no privacy in our home. In this cold house we all lived in the only two warm rooms: the kitchen and the living room. My sister suggested that we take a walk. What a crazy idea that was! Mom was immediately suspicious. With the snow piled high everywhere, the road was the only path where we could walk. As soon as we got away from the house, I told my sister that I was planning to leave the convent. I just blurted it out. I had been waiting for days to tell someone, anyone.

We walked and talked until we couldn't stand the cold another minute. My sister came through for me; she helped me make a plan. I loved my sister for her support. She didn't ask me if I was sure; she didn't question me about how I was going to make it. She just took charge. I told her that I wanted to stay until I graduated. She immediately decided to attend my graduation, and afterwards she would load up my few possessions and bring me back to Denver, where she was living. She said I could stay there as long as I wanted. The plan was set.

The happiness I felt was overwhelming but it was very short lived. We broke the news to Mom as soon as we returned to the house. She was furious, even more upset than when I announced I was going to the convent. She kept repeating: "Good Lord, God bless you." She bombarded me with questions. How could I possibly make it in this world that I had not known for five years? Where was I going to live? How would I support myself? She tried her best to talk me out of my decision. She possibly feared that I might want to return home. But I never once considered that. I wanted to see the world!

I refused to adopt my mother's fears. I had plans to make. I had places to go. On the train I dared to dream a little about what my future life would be. I knew that when I returned to school I needed to apply myself to finishing my last semester of college. I felt like I had a new lease on life. I decided on that train trip that I would never again let myself be depressed. I couldn't imagine that I would ever get married or have children, but I did think about the freedom ahead of me. I could go where I wanted. I could eat what I wanted. I could wear what I wanted. I could shop for clothes. I could live where I wanted. I could deal with God on my own terms.

I didn't know how to process my relationship with God. I had tried so hard during those five years to get close to God. I wanted Him to show up in my life. I was making this extreme sacrifice, but God seemed totally silent. Where was He? Why did I feel so abandoned by Him? The Catholic Church seemed so archaic to me. I wondered why the older nuns stayed in the convent. Perhaps they were too afraid to leave. I wondered why anyone would want to choose this life. I went in the chapel to pray but I had nothing to say. I felt totally abandoned by God. I remember thinking to myself: I have prayed enough these five years to last me the rest of my life. I am taking time off from God. In maybe fifteen or twenty years, I will get back to dealing with this issue. For me it was the deepest crisis in faith. I could hardly wait to not have to go to Mass or any service. I would leave the Catholic Church for good. I had seen it from the inside and I didn't like it. These were some of my thoughts on that long train ride back to school.

That last semester of college was the most exciting of all. I had a new lease on life. I was going to graduate. My dream was coming true for me. The most amazing fact--I was leaving the convent. I whispered to myself in my free time: "I am leaving! I am leaving!" When not studying, I spent time in my room thinking about what my new life would be like. I did tell a few people I was leaving. One of my classmates, Beverly, was an only child from a wealthy Chicago family. When her parents came to visit, Beverly told them about my decision to leave and my complete lack of resources. Her Mom offered me all the clothes she no longer wanted, a number of beautiful outfits from Marshall Field's in Chicago, and twenty dollars in cash. I stared at the clothes. I couldn't imagine wearing a single one of these sophisticated, adult clothes from the North Shore boutiques when kids my age were wearing bell-bottoms and halter tops. I was now twenty-three. After I tried them on, I packed them in my suitcase. At least I would have some color in my black suitcase when I left.

During this last semester of school, I was also student teaching in a fourth-grade classroom of a Catholic elementary school. This was a totally frightening experience for me. I was so ill prepared for student teaching that I spent most of my time just watching. Each time the supervising teacher told me it was now my turn to teach a class, I begged off. I survived the whole semester in this way. I believe I taught only one class during the semester, the day my college professor came to observe. Those students were so good; all I had to do was figure out what to teach during that one period. The supervising teacher helped me by telling me exactly what to say. I practiced it over and over again. The whole experience was unsettling. Teaching didn't feel right. I had made my decision to become a teacher in fourth grade, when I longed to grow up and become the kind of teacher I had needed. Not one teacher in all my years of schooling had encouraged me, seen through my shyness, said that I would make it, that I was smart. That was what I wanted so desperately to hear. I wanted to do that for my students. But my student teaching didn't give me a chance to do any of this. I wondered if it might be different when I got my own class, but I didn't know if I could teach a class all day every day! I put this concern on the "backburner" because my immediate agenda was to graduate, leave the convent, find a place to live and land a job.

The truth was that teaching was the only thing I was prepared to do, and yet I wasn't really prepared although I had just spent the past five years in a teaching order. I decided my only choice was to apply for teaching jobs, but where should I apply--in Iowa, at a Catholic school? About that time, I learned that one of my closest friends, already out on mission, planned to leave. I approached her with the idea of sharing an apartment with me, in a city close to where we both grew up. I thought it was a great idea because we had both led a very sheltered life, so we could find out about the world together. The best thing of all: she was very funny and made me laugh. We could laugh together as we adjusted to our new lives outside the convent. She said "Yes!"

I applied to several nearby Catholic elementary schools, insisting that I was planning to leave the convent but wanted to teach in a Catholic school. (I wasn't able at this point to admit that I had become totally disconnected from God.) I got a call from the principal of a Catholic school with about 300 students, in need of a fourth-grade teacher. That was the grade I had "student taught". The principal interviewed me over the phone. She said she was interested in me because, even though I was leaving the convent, sisters did make the best teachers! The pay--$4,300 per year--sounded like so much money to me. She suggested I visit the school when I got home. (She didn't say: when you leave the convent.) She called me Sister Janice. I wanted to remind her that she would be calling me Miss McDermott, but I would deal with that later.

The day before graduation, I met with the mother superior. She gave me forty dollars to buy some things she thought I would need. She reminded me that my vows were still in force until August, that even though I wasn't in the convent, I must live in poverty, chastity and obedience. In August I could sign the paper terminating my affiliation with the Franciscan Order. I was informed that I must also pay back my tuition expenses because I had failed to go on a mission. This bit of news upset me greatly as I had just given five precious years of my youth to them. I did, however, feel indebted to them for my college education and vowed to make regular contributions to the Motherhouse. I informed them of my intention.

Graduation day arrived. I was so excited. My whole family attended the ceremony. They were there as my name was announced with those students receiving a B.A. in Sociology and Education: Sister Janice McDermott. That would be the last time I heard that name. The day before the ceremony my family had enjoyed a picnic in a nearby park. My sister and I had already finalized the plan for my escape. In my trunk I had stored my habit, shoes, rosaries, prayer books, and small hand-made booklets with poems and quotes from friends that I had saved over the past five years. I would not need anything in that trunk; I would pick it up when my vows expired.

Chapter VII
From Despair to Hope!

It is now more than forty years since I left the convent, and I have spent my adult life studying, researching, reading, praying and writing, in an effort to process my childhood and early adult life. I have moved from despair to the greatest hope. For this reason, I am eager to share my story.

I felt angry, betrayed and confused after I left the convent. I had given five of the most precious years of my life to God, had become a "bride of Christ" and had taken vows of poverty, chastity and obedience. I had left everything and everyone to follow Christ, locked away for five years of praying, silence and studying Holy Scripture. After I left the convent I routinely said: "I prayed enough in those five years to possibly last me for the rest of my life." I had dedicated my life to God, but left the convent feeling alone and lost. It was my decision to leave, but I felt, in many ways, that I had been forced to leave. I no longer felt in tune with what was happening with the church and with God. There was emptiness inside, a void that was too painful to ignore. There was really no other choice but to leave. Why did I feel so abandoned? Because my dream to make my family proud and to live out my religious vocation had collapsed into shambles!

After the ceremony I said goodbye to my family. I changed out of my habit, grabbed my suitcase full of Beverly's mother's clothes and jumped into my sister's car. I did say goodbye to a few people, but all of my classmates were with their families, celebrating their own graduation. We drove all night to her house in Denver where I would begin my new life. I planned to stay with her for awhile.

At the time my sister was working at a radio station. Her manager knew she was going to retrieve her younger sister from a convent and asked if he could interview me on the radio when I arrived in Denver. The interview took place at the radio station three days after I left the convent.

I recently learned that my younger brother still had the reel-to-reel tape with the interview. I asked him to send it to me. I was able to find a company that does archival work, and they played the tape for me for the first time in forty years. I heard myself saying that I found it more difficult to be a Christian in the convent than out of the convent. People expected things from me because I was a nun; that I was unable to mesh who I was as a person with who I was as a nun. I gave the example of how I had strong views on our involvement in the Vietnam War and I had participated in many protest marches; yet we were criticized by members of our religious community for taking such a strong stand against the war. I spoke about dealing with society's changing view of the role of a nun and with the idea of who I wanted to be as a maturing, changing person. I talked about my decision to leave and the joy and freedom I experienced once I made the decision to leave. I talked about how no longer wearing a habit had affected me. I said that wearing the habit didn't make a difference for nuns because it was much more important to focus on what was happening inside each person. I said that wearing a habit did not determine whether people lived a loving life filled with dedication and service. I heard myself saying that the problem was with the older nuns who were resisting changes. I admitted I had learned a lot and enjoyed the experience. I said it seemed no different than going into the Army or Navy and then coming back a changed person. I told the interviewer that I knew life would be hard so I wasn't at all surprised that being in the convent was as hard as it was. I had to admit to myself that this life wasn't working out for me; I had to be strong and courageous enough to make the hard decision to leave. I had to admit to myself that I was not happy. Because I was unhappy I couldn't really help myself or anyone else. I said that it was my fault that I had to leave. I wasn't strong enough to be myself in the community. I said I felt conflicted about going to teach in a Catholic school; I had so much background in the Catholic Church and thought I should share that with the students I would be teaching. The interviewer asked me if I planned to get married if the right man came along. I said I guessed so but I was not at that point looking for a relationship. There were so many things I needed to experience and adjust to before I could think about being in a relationship. I said I would be busy discovering all the things I had missed for the past five years.

The first year after I left the convent was fraught with drama, confusion, and indescribable joy and happiness. (That is another story for another time.) A couple of years after my departure, I met and married a wonderful man who had spent five years in the Christian Brothers. We had a lot in common. We married after a short courtship and had two beautiful daughters. We were crazy about our girls. We felt blessed to have found each other and to have such incredible girls in our lives, but we struggled with our careers, our finances, and our relationship. Every negative situation completely shook us. We were being forced to grow up. It was a painful time. We did not feel settled in our lives. We felt so alone in the world, living far away from family and friends. What was missing? Why were we so frightened by life? How could we live our lives with more joy? Where was the peace I believed we should have?

One day I had a thought that completely changed the way my life would unfold. I thought...... what if I had made the right decision when I left the convent? What if God was actually instrumental in my decision to leave, so that I could begin to create a happy life, meet my husband and live my life blessed with such a loving husband and two great children? In that moment I vowed: *I am going to re-decide*. I am going to start living my life again with faith and the belief that a loving God is at the center of my world, and that this was all part of His grand plan for me: to go to the convent for awhile and then leave. I decided that God was indeed central to leading me to the incredible life I now have. At that point, I began to search for a church that would help me navigate the process of getting to know God in a new light.

I was teaching at a public school in Milwaukee when I asked a teacher on staff whether she had been in the convent. She seemed a bit taken aback by my question, but answered that she had, indeed, been in the convent for many years! We started meeting and talking regularly. She confided in me that she was dating a man who had been a priest. She was struggling with whether she should marry him; he had already been married a number of times. They did eventually get married and started a church called St. Ann's. It was not a Catholic Church although it sounded like one. I started to attend there regularly. My husband did not want any involvement with the church once he left the Christian Brothers, so I took both girls by myself. They attended the meditation/yoga service for children.

This church introduced me to the "New Age Movement". **New Age** is a spiritual movement, developed in the late 19th century, which emphasizes metaphysical beliefs. It is comprised of a group of religious and secular organizations, authors, philosophers, and individuals who share beliefs about positive thinking, the law of attraction, healing, life force, creative visualization and personal power. I was fascinated by these beliefs and began my journey of working with affirmations and positive thinking; I began to see how the law of attraction was working in my life. It was at this church that I made my first vision map, here that I had past life regressions and had my first natal chart reading. I began to consult an astrologer in an effort to try to better understand my life. I had started on a healing path. I began to envision God in a new way, in a very different way from the GOD that I grew up with in the Catholic Church.

For twenty-three years, I had been taught that God was a He, an angry God, a God who punished, who never gave anyone a break. I was not worthy to be in His presence. We were to be punished because we were sinners. He was to be feared! He lived in Heaven which was somewhere up in the sky. Our only hope: to suffer as much as possible on earth so we could save our souls. If we were lucky we would end up in Purgatory. If we suffered enough during our lives, we would earn the right to live in Heaven with Him after we died. He would judge each of us according to how well we lived the Ten Commandments.

My husband and I and our two girls eventually moved to Colorado in 1988, where I have continued my search for a spiritual life. Gradually, I began to change my perceptions about my life. I came to believe that although I was placed in a difficult situation early in my life, I did not have to stay there. As an adult, I was allowed to make my own choices: I had the freedom to change my mind.

I started to understand that I am the creator of my life, and the thoughts I choose to think will create my life. I learned, after waiting so many years for someone to come and help me, that no one could help me create a better life for myself or for our family; it was my life to create as best I could. Part of growing up was to realize that no one would come to rescue me; I had to make it on my own. I had thought that if I complained enough, surely people would feel sorry for me and give me money or other things I needed. (It never happened but I kept trying this for a very long time--too long!)

It took me a long time to accept responsibility for my life, to realize that I was the one who had created this life and if I wasn't satisfied with it, I was the only one who could change it. I started studying the Religious Science philosophy--CHANGE YOUR THINKING, CHANGE YOUR LIFE. I began to work on changing my thinking, so that I could change my life.

I became a student of the "Course in Miracles", a self-study spiritual thought system that teaches that the way to Universal Love is through forgiveness. This course gave me some of my favorite comforting quotes: "If you knew Who walks beside you on the way that you have chosen, fear would be impossible", "Trust would solve all your problems now" and "The way to God is through forgiveness here. There is no other way." And in this study I found the meaning and purpose for the direction of my life's work:

> **"I am here only to be truly helpful.**
> **I am here to represent Him who has sent me.**
> **I do not need to worry about what to say or what to do because He who sent me will direct me.**
> **I am content to be wherever He wishes knowing that He will go there with me.**
> **I will be healed as I let Him teach me to heal."**

Used with permission of the Foundation for Inner Peace.

I learned that there is a power for good in the universe far greater than myself, and I have learned to use this great power. Do I understand it? NO! Do I believe there are spiritual guides working overtime to help me stay on my path? YES. Some call it Source Energy or your Higher Power.

I continue to strive to be aware of both my ways of thinking and the stories I tell myself. Every year I recommit to this practice, examining the stories on a deeper level and with impeccable vigilance because I know my old programming can seep in when I am not paying attention.

I recently commented to my husband about a realtor who sends us a calendar every year with a picture of her annual trip to some exotic place. This year she was on a camel with the Pyramids in the background. I heard myself saying: "She must make tons of money to take trips like that every year." My loving husband said: "Yes, she does make a lot of money but she works very, very hard." Almost immediately I realized that my old programming was rising up again. My new story reflects my happiness for her good fortune and her success, and that she is able to enjoy the money she has worked so hard to make.

Today I live my life with a focus on service. Each day I ask Source Energy this question: HOW CAN I HELP? HOW CAN I SERVE? Here are some of the tools I use to help me stay focused on my life's work. I use them daily to build a spiritual focus to my life.

Affirmations: An affirmation is a carefully formatted statement that is repeated to one's self and written down frequently. For an affirmation to be effective, it must be in the present tense, positive, personal and specific. I love repeating positive affirmations throughout the day. I carry them in my pocket and pull them out whenever I have a few minutes to relax and refocus….. usually when I am stuck in traffic or waiting in line at the grocery store. A list of my favorite affirmations is included in the Appendix.

Abundance: Abundance is **a sufficient quantity or supply of all that you need.** I continue to push past the barriers of my early programming regarding money, that invisible wall that tries to prevent me from moving to the new level of abundance. I know that wealth is a state of consciousness, and I want to expand my consciousness to increase the divine supply flowing into my life. I know that money is energy and that the more I share, the more I will receive. You can give only to yourself because everything that you give comes back to you multiplied. Saying affirmations related to money helps me to focus on being willing to accept all the good that Source Energy has planned for me. I have included my favorite prosperity affirmations in the Appendix.

Surrender: To surrender means to yield ownership, to relinquish control over what we consider to be ours: our property, our time and our "rights". By surrendering to Source Energy, we admit that He/She is ultimately in control of everything, including our present circumstances. What we resist will persist. How does it look? When surrendering you make the intention to step back, to step way back so that God can take over. You admit that you have tried everything but you simply can't figure it out so you are turning it over to God.

Gratitude: Gratitude is an attitude that acknowledges that we are thankful or appreciative of all that we have received or will receive. I have learned that the way to live a joyful life is to be grateful for everything in my life. I have kept a gratitude journal for many years. Every day I write at least five things for which I am grateful. I also record five things I love and admire about myself. What are some of the things I am grateful for? It is very easy to look at your day and be grateful for the incredible blessings of each day. Our days are filled with things we often take for granted. For instance, one of the things I find myself continually grateful for is my garage. Every time I drive into my garage, I say a little prayer of thanksgiving for it. I am so grateful I have a place inside to park my car. This grateful thought comes from all those years of cold, snowy winters lived in Milwaukee, where we had to park our car halfway down the block, and then carry our groceries and children through the freezing cold. Another thing I am continually grateful for is our bathrooms. I am so grateful to be able to use the bathroom inside and then simply flush the toilet. If I am having a challenging day, I ask myself what I am grateful for; remembering those things helps to shift my energy. Look in the Appendix for a partial list of the things for which I am so deeply grateful.

Loving Myself: This is my most important life lesson, one I did not learn early in my life. My mother could not teach me what she didn't know herself. I do not blame my mother. (She has been dead for twenty-two years.) She wanted perfection but it was and is an impossible expectation in life. Today, I know that I am the only thinker in my head. I no longer let my Mom's voice live there so loudly. On another level, I do believe that I chose to learn my life lessons from my parents, so their parenting was perfect for me. I continue to work on loving and accepting myself, so I write five things every day that I love and admire about myself. This exercise is one way of focusing on the good I have created in my life. I often ask myself these questions: Am I telling myself the truth right now? Am I focused on what I want from life? Am I minding my own business or am I in someone else's business or even in God's business?

Forgiveness: Forgiveness is the process of letting go of resentment, indignation or anger as a result of a **perceived** offense, difference or mistake. "Perceived" is the most important characteristic to notice. We often "make up" stories about what we think happened to us. Sometimes these stories are far from the real truth. I have set the intention to forgive myself daily, as well as forgiving anyone in my life who is in need of forgiveness. Forgiveness releases us from the past, and I have learned that when my life is "stuck" or not flowing well, it usually means that I am holding on to a past situation--regret, sadness, hurt, fear, guilt, blame, anger or resentment. Each of these emotions sprouts from a state of unforgiveness, a refusal to let the past go and move into the present moment. Love is always the answer to healing of any sort..... and the pathway to love is forgiving all those you perceive to have wronged you. You can sit quietly and say: "The person I need to forgive is _____ and I forgive you for _____ ." You will feel lighter as you practice this exercise.

Hope: There are many world and societal problems that dominate our headlines and can preoccupy our minds if we let them. Many feel that the world is getting worse with each passing year. Having hope means that we know that we do have control over our individual lives and that they can be turned around in an instant by simply changing the way we think. We can change our thinking by giving up our need to blame others or to judge them. We can stop focusing on our current situation and focus instead on what our heart is telling us; each loving thought can bring hope and peace to our world. If you have hope, everything else will eventually unfold in perfect order.

Emotional Freedom Technique (EFT): This tapping technique combines Mind/Body Medicine and Acupuncture (without needles). EFT is an emotional version of acupuncture in which certain meridian points are stimulated by tapping on them with your fingertips. The tapping addresses the cause of emotional issues which is unbalanced energy meridians. Emotional stress can contribute to pain, disease and physical ailments. EFT has provided astonishing physical relief as well as emotional relief. I use EFT technique whenever I feel unbalanced, fearful, upset or worried about an issue that has surfaced in my life. It immediately helps me to be more relaxed. You can find out how to tap for various issues at http://www.emofree.com/. This tapping sequence can be used on everything. For instance, if I am feeling concerned about attracting more abundance in my life, I tap for that: "Even though in the past I believed lots of negative programming about money, I deeply and completely love, accept and forgive myself." The tapping points are the same for every issue. You can quickly learn them by watching Brad Yates's YouTube video: http://www.youtube.com/watch?v=aoSzivsQkVI

The Course in Miracles: The course is a self-study spiritual curriculum that integrates forgiveness and its practical application in daily living. There is no author listed on the publication. However, in the preface, Helen Schucman claims to have written the material, with the help of William Thetford, based on an inner voice Schucman identifies as Jesus. From the course I have learned that there is no order of difficulty in miracles, that miracles occur naturally as expressions of love. If I perceive love in others, I am strengthening love in myself. The course teaches that we have a choice: we can live in love or in fear. I have learned that all forgiveness is a gift to myself. I know it is quite possible to reach God; in fact it is the most natural thing in the world. In quietness all things are answered, and every problem is quietly resolved. One of the best, most comforting thoughts is that it is not hard to do the task God has appointed you to do, since it is He who does it. When you have learned to decide with God, all decisions become as easy and as right as breathing. Finally, no one is where he is by accident and chance plays no part in God's plan.

And so I conclude this book with a prayer from Louise Hay:

> "In the infinity of life where I am
> All is perfect, whole and complete.
> The past has no power over me
> because I am willing to learn and change.
> I see the past as necessary to bring me to where I am today.
> I am willing to begin where I am right now.
> I am willing to set myself free.
> All is well in my world."
>
> Used with permission of Louise L. Hay,
> author of *You Can Heal Your Life*.

Janice McDermott

The Optimist Creed

Promise yourself

To be so strong that nothing can disturb your peace of mind.

To talk health, happiness, and prosperity to every person you meet.

To make all your friends feel that there is something worthwhile in them.

To look at the sunny side of everything and make your optimism come true.

To think only of the best, to work only for the best and to expect only the best.

To be just as enthusiastic about the success of others as you are about your own.

To forget the mistakes of the past and press on to the greater achievements of the future.

To wear a cheerful expression at all times and give a smile to every living creature you meet.

To give so much time to improving yourself that you have no time to criticize others.

To be too large for worry, too noble for anger, too strong for fear, and too happy to permit the presence of trouble.

To think well of yourself and to proclaim this fact to the world, not in loud word, but in great deeds.

To live in the faith that the whole world is on your side, so long as you are true to the best that is in you.

(From the "The Optimist Creed" published in 1912 in the book, *Your Forces and How to Use Them* by Christian D. Larson.)

Afterword

It is now 2010 and I am sixty-three. I married an incredibly loving man who loved me back to health. We had two beautiful girls who have brought us more joy than we could have ever thought would be possible. The oldest one is married and has two darling sons. Our youngest daughter recently married a wonderful man. Our oldest recently completed her Master's Degree in Library Science and the youngest daughter, her Master's Degree in Art Therapy last year.

As for me, I am in the process of creating a whole new life for myself. I taught elementary school for twenty-nine years--almost exclusively in the inner cities of Milwaukee and Denver. I took the Montessori Training Course. I completed a Master's degree in Curriculum and Instruction. For a number of years I was the Director of a Huntington Learning Center, an individualized tutoring business that provides additional educational support for kids and adults who need more intensive interventions than those available at school. I worked for eight years at the Colorado Department of Education (CDE). Before leaving CDE I began to work with a life coach. He encouraged me to study to become a life coach as well. After graduating from the life coaching program at Coach University several years ago, I have been building my life coaching business and clarifying where my passion lies. Because of my very early commitment to being the kind of teacher I never had, I am passionate about making sure every educator is focused on giving each student hope, the fighting chance at a good life that a good education can provide. My life coaching has transformed into leadership coaching for school administrators. I am inspired by the knowledge that teachers will be more effective if they have passionate administrators leading their schools.

My Mom has been dead for twenty-three years. She died at age 76 of uterine cancer. After exploratory surgery, she found out she was filled with cancer and lived only three more days. She was clear that she was ready to go. She had always said she did not want to be a burden to anyone, and she definitely felt strongly about not ever living in a nursing home!

My older sister has traveled the world. She continues to amaze us. She speaks five languages fluently and has taught in South Korea, Turkey, Germany and the United States. She is now teaching courses at two different colleges and writing ACT test questions. She has also purchased our family home and remodeled it, and we all enjoy going back to Iowa when we can.

My younger sister has also traveled extensively and only recently moved back to the United States. She and her husband have taught in Germany, Switzerland and France. They now reside in Florida, to allow their four children to finish their college educations and go to law school and medical school. She has two undergraduate degrees and is completing a Ph.D. in Educational Leadership.

My brother who was born the same year as me went to Thailand during the Vietnam War where he worked as a jet mechanic. After his tour of duty, he returned to our home town, working for John Deere for a couple of years. There he built a home one mile from our family home, married a teacher from South Dakota and worked as a Public Works Superintendent. He recently retired from that position.

My youngest brother dropped out of college and moved to Denver to start his own construction company. When he realized his body would eventually wear out, he bought property in the mountains, where he worked evenings and weekends to build a beautiful home. He sold the house, making enough money to return to school full time. He studied to be a CPA and is now the State Controller. He signs every state employee's pay check, even that of the governor.

Finally, as for my convent class, there are five sisters who still live in the convent. A few years ago I got a strange email message: ARE YOU THE JANICE MCDERMOTT THAT LIVED IN DUBUQUE IOWA FROM 1965-1968? I responded immediately. My long-lost friend had been "Googling" former convent classmates. She found many of our classmates so we started communicating regularly. She had learned that one of our classmates was the principal of a Catholic school close to where I lived. We eventually had a reunion of our class at the Motherhouse. It was an amazing experience to reconnect with all those beautiful women with whom I had shared so much of my young life. We talked about so many things: why we went to the convent, why we left, when we left and what had happened to us since we last saw each other. Most of us have married, had children and are now enjoying our grandchildren. The five sisters who stayed in the convent told of their many adventures and their work with the poor in different parts of the country and the world. It was a grand reunion indeed!

Appendix

My favorite affirmations:

- All is well in my life. I am safe.
- I am perfect, whole and complete.
- The point of power is always in the present moment.
- I give myself permission to prosper.
- I am at ease with the changes in my life.
- I do work that I love and I am well paid for it.
- My thinking is peaceful, calm and centered.
- I am kind, gentle and patient with myself.
- I forgive everything and everyone, including myself.
- I live in the present moment and easily release all past pain.
- I take time every day to count my blessings.
- I am so grateful for my life just as it is.
- It is safe for me to grow up.
- I am open and receptive to all the good available to me.
- Life is simple. What I give out I get back.
- Every door is open.
- I claim my own power and I lovingly create my own reality.
- I am constantly creating more good in my life.
- I rejoice in my good health. I love my body and my body loves me.
- I make right decisions quickly because I trust my inner guidance.
- I recognize my body as a wondrous machine. I feel privileged to live in it.
- I release all criticism and blame.
- The entire universe is supporting me.
- I am so grateful for my life and for all that I have.

- I am the most important person in my life.
- All is well in my world.
- I am perfect just as I am.
- My energy is radiant and peaceful.
- There is a Power and Intelligence greater than me and I can use it.
- I have a bright mind. I am a smart person. I learn quickly and easily.
- Whatever I need to know is revealed to me in the right time/space sequence.
- I accept perfect health as a natural state of being.
- I accept all opportunities when they come. I feel confident about my future.
- I am a blessing to the world.
- All of my past except its beauty is gone; nothing is left but a blessing.
- I am now becoming all that I was created to be.
- I surround myself with positive people. I live in a world of love.
- I am neither too little nor too much. I do not have to prove myself to anyone.
- When I listen to my inner self, I hear the answers I need.
- I speak up for myself. I am secure in my own worth.
- I am as successful as I make up my mind to be.
- Source Energy is the only source of my supply.
- I forgive all those needing forgiveness and I forgive myself.
- I slow down and take time to really enjoy my life.
- I am a blessing at home, at work and at play.
- My thoughts are loving.
- I now tap into the unlimited Universe.
- I recommit to staying present in each moment.
- I choose joy and peace all day long.
- I open my heart and let the love dissolve the fear.
- My uniqueness is a gift to the world.
- I have everything I need to be successful.
- I am filled with positive energy.
- I open the door to more good in my life.
- I let go of all fear as I handle my challenges.
- I am a gift and a blessing to the world.
- I lovingly support myself as I learn new skills.

- I am here for myself.
- I praise myself for the big and little things I do.
- I am on my way to consistently loving myself.
- I am the treasure I have been looking for.
- I appreciate the beautiful world I live in.
- I imagine a peaceful planet with all people with an open heart.
- It is safe to love everyone on the planet.
- I live in the moment. Now is all there is.
- I find beauty all around me.
- I am at peace with the perfect unfoldment of my life.
- I love my car and fill it with love wherever I go.
- I select healthy, nutritious food to eat.
- I release the need to be perfect.
- I release old habits with love.
- I am yearning to love all parts of me.
- I am so close to that which I desire.
- Every day I find it easier to give myself unconditional love.
- I am my own best friend.
- I now discover new ways to live my life.
- I surround my family with love and know that good is with them.
- Peace begins with me.
- I choose thoughts that make me feel good, thoughts of gratitude and appreciation.
- I trust the Universe to find the perfect solution.
- Out of this situation only good can come.
- Whatever I need is available to me right now.
- Your will be done.
- I now experience a good beyond my wildest dreams.
- Enlightenment is my 24-hour-a-day job.
- Only good surrounds me and only good comes to me.
- I celebrate my life.
- I keep my thoughts open to new experiences and opportunities.
- Love is stronger than any differences.
- Every breath is bringing perfection, wholeness and renewing every cell.
- I trust Source Energy to resolve every situation.
- There is all the time in the world.

- I am one with the Universal Mind.
- My work is a stepping stone to a far greater expression of Spirit.
- I am now more successful than I could ever imagine.
- I now welcome more love into my life.
- My best is good enough.
- I choose to make this day the happiest day of my life.
- I let every thought of discord float away.
- I am filled with gratitude for what has been and what is now.

My favorite prosperity affirmations:

- I am a money magnet.
- I always have more than enough money.
- There is plenty. There is plenty for all.
- It is okay for me and others to bring in money without working hard.
- I keep my mind focused on serving God.
- God is with me in the region of my heart.
- It is perfectly okay for me to prosper.
- It is perfectly right for me to receive.
- I can trust myself.
- I am on a mission for God. God is my source.
- I can accomplish anything I desire.
- I can fulfill my heart's desire.
- I can trust myself to make good decisions.
- I am a wealthy child of God.
- I am always in the right place at the right time.
- People love giving me gifts.
- I am ready, willing and committed to taking action to create financial well being.
- I am willing to let go of beliefs that create lack and limitation for me.
- I give myself permission to have large sums of money in my life.
- I love money and welcome it into my life.
- God is my immediate, limitless, boundless source of money.
- I am worthy and deserving of all the richness and goodness of life and I claim it now.
- I forgive myself and others for any perceived hurts of the past.

- My consciousness for wealth is expanding each day.
- I am taking action today to decrease my expenses and increase my income.
- I am a generous giver and a gracious receiver of all good things.
- I am a good steward of my financial resources.
- I am proactive and creative in increasing my income.
- I am becoming abundantly prosperous and wealthy.
- I am compelled to see every opportunity that presents itself.
- I now say YES to unlimited abundance.
- Every cell in my body surrenders to Spirit's unlimited power.
- My income is constantly expanding.
- Today I open my heart to more good in my life.
- I accept my abundance.
- I open the door to more good in my life.
- I step aside and let abundance manifest itself.

My surrender affirmations:

- I know that in each moment I am free to decide.
- No matter how much I protest, I am totally responsible for everything that happens to me.
- My past is nothing more than the trail I have left behind. What drives my life today is the energy I generate in each of my present moments.
- I rid myself of my doubts by remembering that there is a valid reason for everything that happens to me.
- I realize that I am always free to let go and observe my life.
- The more I listen, the more profound the silence becomes.
- I know that my highest self is always ready to lift me up beyond the world I experience with my senses.
- I know I can connect my mind with the Divine Mind and guarantee myself peace in every moment.
- I know I am strengthened as I seek to make truth my personal reality.
- I know that the very essence of my being and the way to transform my life is love.
- My judgments keep me from seeing the good that lies behind appearances.

- I know I am already whole and do not need to chase after anything to be complete.
- I do not need to dominate anyone in order to be spiritually awake.
- I will work this day at my purest intentions for the highest good of all.
- I will radiate my sacred self outward for the collective good of all.

My gratitude list:

- For Debby Bernau for helping me edit my book and being so positive about it
- For my yoga class
- For the furnace coming on this morning
- For the many clothes in my closet
- For this beautiful morning
- For the birds singing as I look out my window
- For the Buddhist chant playing on my CD player
- For our beautiful daughters and their partners
- For having Spirit help me write this chapter
- For sunshine
- For the birds coming to the bird feeder
- For the delicious dinner I prepared
- For Judy Collins' voice
- For our daughter's strong confidence in her presentation last night
- For my chance to surrender and let go
- For being willing to trust the Universe
- For the peace in my heart
- For my own inner strength
- For the gift of a reliable car
- For my life-coaching clients
- For the time to relax and enjoy each day
- For my commitment to being a loving presence in the world
- For accepting my life exactly the way it is
- For knowing and being willing to tell my truth
- For my perfect health

- For my glorious future
- For our extended family in Denver
- For our trip to Iowa to see our loving family
- For my husband's wisdom and love
- For the abundance of money in my life
- For getting to spend time with our two grandsons
- For our bathrooms
- For all the appliances in our home that work so well
- For our home that provides us with shelter and protection
- For the wildlife that live by our small lake
- For a beautiful view of the mountains and the lake
- For the gift of silence
- For my willingness to write even when I don't want to
- For the rains that have come to make our grass and plants so green
- For the pain I feel because it is teaching me to go within and watch my thinking
- For the promise of each new day
- For believing even when I don't see any evidence
- For trusting the process
- For getting to walk regularly with my friend
- For knowing there is Divine Timing with every situation
- For knowing my gifts and being willing to share them with the world
- For getting to work with a district to support their administrators
- For time alone
- For being willing to take care of myself
- For my unique path to discover my gifts
- For getting to work at the Colorado Department of Education for 8 years
- For my computer and printer
- For being introduced to the Emotional Freedom Technique (EFT) and using it regularly to heal my life
- For the dream of publishing my memoir
- For my deep spiritual connection with Source Energy
- For the teachings of Jerry and Esther Hicks

A sample list of what I love and admire about myself:

- I love and admire myself for knowing that Spirit is closer to me than I am to myself.
- I love and admire myself for learning the Emotional Freedom Technique (EFT) and using it when I am challenged.
- I love and admire myself for expecting miracles and acknowledging them when they occur.
- I love and admire myself for doing yoga regularly.
- I love and admire myself for following through on my commitments.
- I love and admire myself for taking such good care of my body.
- I love and admire myself for my fresh face showing an aliveness and joy never before experienced.
- I love and admire myself for being courageous enough to start my coaching business.
- I love and admire myself for how I watch my thoughts and the story I am creating.
- I love and admire myself for being willing to create a new story.
- I love and admire myself for marrying my husband and continuing to work on improving our relationship.
- I love and admire myself for helping to create two incredible children who are making a huge difference in the world.
- I love and admire myself for staying open to Spirit's guidance.
- I love and admire myself for trusting in the big dreams I have created.
- I love and admire myself for trusting the process even when things don't seem like they are working out correctly.
- I love and admire myself for my gorgeous blue eyes.
- I love and admire myself for loving what is.
- I love and admire myself for knowing that God is working in my life as me.
- I love and admire myself for going out of my way to help friends and family.
- I love and admire myself for my dreams of helping to heal the planet through my writing and coaching.

- I love and admire myself for being myself and not making excuses for being me.
- I love and admire myself for asking for and receiving amazing grace each day of my life.
- I love and admire myself for being willing to change and grow.
- I love and admire myself for knowing that it is my mind that establishes everything that happens to me.
- I love and admire myself for living my life as if everything was a miracle.
- I love and admire myself for letting go of my agenda for Spirit's magnificent adventure.

LaVergne, TN USA
19 March 2011
220760LV00002B/4/P